Advance

It's not often tha~~t~~
read this account,
the commitment of these precious ambassadors for the Lord is
indeed awe-inspiring—their commitment came at great cost and
returned little in financial success. Yet, their passion seems unre-
strained. To realize how many lives have been changed through
their ministry makes me wonder what would happen in our own
communities if we showed even part of the commitment and enthusiasm for sharing the Good News. The information in this volume should be shared with every believer in the western world.

—Ruth Smith Meyer, Ailsa Craig, Ontario
Author, *Books that Inspire*

Ten years ago, Mark Noll and Carolyn Nystrom released a book
titled *Clouds of Witnesses: Christian Voices from Africa and Asia*. One
of their basic contentions is that we need more stories of Christians from the Majority World. *Light Shining into Darkness* helps to
meet this need. These stories from the Indian subcontinent illustrate the vitality of God's church around the world. Brian Stewart
(CBC international reporter) has described his surprise at finding
so many outposts of what he calls "muscular Christianity" around
the world. Philemon and Kirit are examples of God's presence
working in and through God's people in a "muscular" or powerful way. Debates about social action versus evangelism, or about
the place of power encounter in evangelism, melt away in the fire
of their own experience of God's call and God's power. I invite
you to enjoy—and to learn from and imitate—the experience of

these two (and others whose stories appear alongside them) as you read this book.

—Daryl Climenhaga, Steinbach, Manitoba
Associate Professor, Global Studies
Providence University College and Seminary

LIGHT

SHINING INTO DARKNESS

COMPILED BY ENGAGE STAFF

LIGHT SHINING INTO DARKNESS
Copyright © 2021 by Engage Today

The content of this publication is based on actual events. Names may have been changed to protect individual privacy.

For more information about the ministries in this book, and/or to learn more about how to partner with them through prayer or financial giving, please contact:

Engage Today
Phone: 204-957-8784
Email: office@engage.today
Website: www.engage.today

Printed in Canada

Print ISBN: 978-1-4866-1662-6
eBook ISBN: 978-1-4866-1663-3

Word Alive Press
119 De Baets Street, Winnipeg, MB R2J 3R9
www.wordalivepress.ca

MIX
Paper from
responsible sources
FSC® C103567

Cataloguing in Publication may be obtained through Library and Archives Canada

Contents

COMPILER'S PREFACE

As the overseeing of the editing and shaping of these stories has come to fruition, my hope is that the reader will gain a feel of God's work around the world. The purpose of this book is much the same as that of our organization: to reach the unreached parts of the world with the story of Jesus, and to come alongside those who are already doing this work in their own country. We come alongside our indigenous friends to encourage them in their work—after all, they are the ones who can answer their neighbours' questions about their life and purpose in a culturally appropriate manner at the right time and place. May this book encourage you, in your neighbourhood, to do the same with your neighbours!

We also hope that our readers will come alongside our indigenous friends: to pray and to be part of their initiatives as opportunity allows; to be part of God's team doing God's work in God's ways around the globe.

These stories are our way of allowing you to meet two of our long-time friends the way we ourselves first met them, hearing the stories told as we met in our living room and at the dining table. We have edited them for clarity and understanding to make them easier for you to read. So sit in a comfortable chair and read as if you were listening to them on the other side of your room.

A few years ago, Philemon sat on my living room couch and expanded on the story I'd first heard ten years ago on one of his visits here. He began with his testimony, but he also told me about others who had served before him, and then about how God worked in his life a step at a time. Over time, especially as I rode with him down mountain highways, I also heard more details, especially about two men who have come alongside him at different times in different ways, and how God multiplied the work according to His own plans.

Philemon describes opportunities in his life that he hadn't considered before, and how they were entered into each time first with prayer and then with action. All of the people in the stories in this book have been involved in amazing things, but it is apparent that this isn't because they are so gifted, nor because they had adequate resources, but because they said "Yes!" when God gave them an opportunity. This allowed God to equip them for their unique tasks.

You will read about Bakht Singh (who came to Christ in Winnipeg!) and Prem, and then Dhan, Habil, and others who have worked both with and alongside Philemon. These other threads came from Philemon's testimony, and they thrilled my heart as I was drawn to think of how God weaves a tapestry to carry out His work in His way. I also spent time personally with Dhan and Habil, allowing me to delve further into their ministries and see the story through their eyes.

Philemon's story is written in mixed first and third person, like a biographical narrated story with some overlapping sections that reveal parts of the other stories while concentrating on Philemon as the core.

I first heard Kirit's story through other staff who had travelled with him in his country. Later he came to our office in Canada twice, and even to my home, giving me the opportunity to gradually take in more of the picture. Kirit tells us about yet another area, another culture, another set of challenges from God; this story is an account of a man and his wife who said "Yes" to these challenges instead of accepting other invitations that would have given personal wealth and fame. Kirit is a man who gets up very early to pray—here as at home—and a man who is always bringing Jesus into the picture. I heard about how he learned to reach his own people—this man who is concerned to get the Word out in the language of those people. I then heard about him reaching out to another people, not his own, because God impressed this on his heart. Kirit has also taken on the challenge of unifying the church of Christ to get the task done. Imagine finding a strategy to reach out to eight districts—to as many people as live in our Canadian prairies—and actually finding a way to carry it out in a few years, using trusted compatriots so it is done personally.

Kirit's story is written by a fellow staff member as a narrative, to bring out the main characteristics of this godly man and his impact on his state.

Each of these men has said "Yes!" to their Lord. Each reveals a deep heart for God and a great effect on many others. We have seen this effect firsthand as we have come alongside them in leadership seminars, and have seen them working with other leaders in their networks and organizations. These stories are as diverse as are their cultures.

We have stated the actual names of the countries, larger cities, and main characters where it was appropriate. But we have used pseudonyms for most of the other people and for some towns and areas to prevent unwanted attention in restricted access countries. We know that God knows who each of the characters are; when you pray, He knows who you are praying for. We pray that the true stories in this book will encourage you, grip your heart, and add to the fire that is the Holy Spirit in you. What an opportunity to pray for these others as you read these pages!

FOREWORD

I swim almost every day, and while I swim, I pray. Because of five knee operations, I swim like a sea dog. A hockey injury barely healed before my knee was reinjured in football, leading to several surgeries. Then I broke off part of my kneecap in a farm accident. I can walk without a limp, as long as I swim. Swimming is the best exercise for me, especially with flippers. Therefore, I can be found many days motoring back and forth at the local pool. I am like an otter or a sea dog on my back, keeping up with just about anyone swimming beside me.

I refer to the uninterrupted sixty minutes I spend swimming as my "Hour of Prayer." One day I was concentrating my prayer focus on a country in Southeast Asia that I would soon be visiting. I cried out to the Lord, "How can I prepare for an event like this?" It was to be my first time presenting at a leadership seminar. Our sister organization in the United States, ANM, had invited me to be a part of a team of four speakers for a three-day conference. "How can I relate to the believers in the most densely populated country in the world? They make one dollar a day and face perpetual vulnerability to ravaging storms." On and on I prayed.

Then the Spirit of Christ ministered to me with the message, "You are going to this place to love them. All other objectives are secondary. I will empower you to walk with them and to come alongside them."

Immediately I was filled with joy. I knew I could love them with the love of the Lord. As I swam back and forth, my lane became a sanctuary to sing His praises in my heart. I left the pool that day entirely satisfied that I knew what I would do.

—Brother David

WHY START A NEW MISSION TO WORK WITH INDIGENOUS MISSIONS ORGANIZATIONS?

The evangelical movement in the world has changed. At one time, evangelism, church planting, and discipleship were mission endeavours primarily undertaken by the Church in the West; but now, they are distinctive marks of the Indigenous Church in many pockets of the world. The Good News of Jesus Christ is bearing fruit as indigenous Christians faithfully spread the Gospel. Movements are gaining momentum as the Gospel takes root. Engage Today (ENGAGE) was birthed to come alongside indigenous church planting ministries that are reaching out to unreached people groups, and to help them to equip the Church for works of service.

WITH WHOM DOES ENGAGE WORK?

ENGAGE works primarily with the leaders of independent indigenous mission groups. By visiting the indigenous missions and building relationships with them, ENGAGE has come to know our indigenous mission leaders. Our vision of discipleship is serving in suitable and appropriate ways, and encouraging the indigenous mission in their lead ministry role. The indigenous missions we work with: 1) demonstrate a burden for the lost and a commitment to building the Church, 2) have a clear evangelical statement of faith, 3) are faithful in the face of spiritual and physical opposition, 4) are committed to financial transparency, and 5) serve under the accountability of a board of directors. ENGAGE is inspired by our indigenous partners mostly because they are committed followers of Jesus Christ. They know the Bible has commissioned believers to *"Go into all the world and make disciples"* (Matthew 28:19, paraphrased), and they are determined to walk in obedience regardless of the obstacles and challenges that they face.

PHILEMON'S STORY

MEETING PHILEMON

Philemon and Elishiba first came to Canada in 2008 during an ENGAGE visit. I was involved both in a staff barbecue and a local event where I heard Philemon's testimony and met both him and his wife.

In 2015 I worked with him much more directly. I was involved with helping him with a visa matter so he could come to our country, and also in advocating for earthquake relief to some of those in his care. (The 2015 earthquake struck a week after he was at our house.) Philemon and I had spent more than a week together in our house and on the road. Every day I learned more of his story.

In Nepal in 2016, on a two-day retreat with Philemon, I learned about Habil and his son, Toshan, and actually got to meet them. Highlights of that trip included riding an elephant, a jungle jeep, and a hollowed-out log canoe with Habil, and having two hours of question and answer time about his life. I also spent some time with Philemon, visiting in his home, seeing two other ministries, and preaching in his church.

In 2017, I again visited Philemon, but this time conducted a pastoral retreat in one of Habil's areas along with a group from Philemon's own church. I also visited again in early 2018 for a seminar and encouragement time, and have added three additional updates that I feel are helpful to the story.

It is with great joy that I bring you this account! Philemon is a partner who we feel needs to be known across Canada, a partner who needs prayer and resources for his Nepal-wide teaching on radio and TV, and whose church planting pastors and supervisors could also use a helping hand. Read and rejoice about how, as a new convert, Philemon was so excited he started preaching before becoming a teenager! Note his dedication to the task, and the excitement as he is joined by others to minister in far places in his country! And consider his heart as he is involved in counselling politicians, and in advocating for Christians in his country. Pray, and if the Lord leads you, ask yourself how you might be further involved in his ministry!

—Brother Bruce

PHILEMON: TIMELINE

About 1955–56: birth (records were not kept well in Nepal)

1960: Mother passes away

1965: Philemon begins school

1968–70: Lives with Prem

1971: Begins ministry

1972–87: Ministers with Pastor David (often staying with him too)

1973–76: Attends Bible school

1983–1991: Father lives with Philemon

1985: Gets married

1992: Starts a church in Prem's new school

1996: Moves to work in Nepal

1998: Becomes leader of Prem's non-school mission work

2008: Radio ministry begins

2009: TV ministry begins

In Nepal, the scenery is spectacular, but avalanches and mud slides frequently block the roads.

PHILEMON'S STORY

This is the story of how God led Philemon to Himself, prepared him for ministry, and has faithfully been with him and his ministry team as he follows God's call.

SIMPLE BEGINNINGS OF MINISTRY

Bursting with the Gospel of his Lord Jesus Christ, Philemon returned from Bible school. As a young graduate, he started doing full time ministry in the hills of Darjeeling, going from place to place, and holding open-air meetings, especially in the tea garden villages. People were so hungry for the Word of God that wherever he and his team preached the Gospel, there was a readiness to accept the Lord. But in some places the team also faced problems, like the threat of stoning from people who were against their preaching.

Philemon did not count the years, as they went by quickly. During these years he didn't have his own room to stay in. But he did have a place to sleep. Pastor David's dining table provided a daily place of rest for most of those years. It was simply not possible to sleep on the floor due to the heavy dampness and cold in the hills of Darjeeling. Sleeping on the table meant Philemon had to wait until he and the others had finished eating their evening meals and cleaned up; sometimes it was 11:00 at night before he could go to sleep. In the morning, he would wrap up his bed roll and put it in someone's room. And then after eating, he would go along with Pastor David on his evangelistic journeys or preach himself day after day. This ministry continued for about twelve years.

So these are the simple beginnings of Philemon's ministry. He rejoiced because the Lord Himself was with him wherever he was. Like Paul, Philemon praised God for His promises and care. Here is Philemon's testimony of the conversion of his uncle, father and himself, in his own words.

PART ONE: PHILEMON'S FAMILY FINDS JESUS

PHILEMON SPEAKS: MY FAMILY BACKGROUND

The Lord miraculously called me out of an orthodox Hindu background. My father was a Hindu guru known as a *shadhu*, and my grandfather was a witch doctor. Both of them were well-respected men in Hindu society. We lived in the Gaurishankar hill region of Nepal, a couple of valleys west from Mt. Everest.

While fighting for the Indian army during World War II, my father was wounded in an explosion in Rome.

He lost his right leg on the spot. Most of his friends walked away, thinking he was dead, but one of them said, "Let's take him to the hospital." By the grace of God, a year later he had been healed. Though my father wasn't a Christian at the time, God had spared his life.

After he returned home with one leg, he married my mother. She gave birth to five children, but four died and I was only one that was left. Finally, she also died, leaving me motherless at the age of four. After my mother died, my father, with his one leg, raised me alone, giving me the love of both father and mother.

My father was very religious. Every day, he would get up at sunrise and do his *puja* to his gods and goddesses (which involved worship and care of the images). He would also do this at noon, sunset and midnight to make sure the deities would not abandon the place they had appeared. He believed that his gods lived in temples, in homes, and in outdoor public spaces. He also used to arrange a religious gathering every month where people would read through Hindu books together. As his son, I followed his footsteps in worshipping idols, walking after him when he would go to worship his gods.

MY UNCLE CAME HOME PROFESSING CHRIST

When I was about nine years old, my uncle returned home having accepted Christ as his personal Saviour. My uncle had gone on a long journey east to Kalimpong, just over the border into India, because he suspected he had tuberculosis, which was considered incurable at that time. He wanted some treatment so he might at least live longer.

Some Christian nurses from a Scottish Presbyterian church associated with the Christian hospital in Darjeeling witnessed to my uncle about the Lord Jesus Christ while he was being treated. It wasn't long before he accepted Christ as his personal Saviour. This hospital was a very good tool to reach Nepali people who crossed the border for medical help there.

My uncle was told that everyone in the village rejected him when they heard that he had changed his religion, so he waited over a year before returning. He spent this time leading people to the Lord in the Darjeeling area and preaching at local churches. Having become a Christian, he became worse than untouchable[1] to his fellow villagers. People in his village were even thinking of preventing him from returning to Nepal, his home country. But finally his family, wife and daughters urged him to return anyway, whatever might happen. When he came home, the village authority had a meeting and wanted to send him back to India. But his oldest brother objected, saying his brother had already been regarded as dead to them and they really wanted him to be able to stay even if he was considered as low caste now.

The area chief had warned my uncle, saying that he had to leave the village within twenty-four hours. But to his surprise, the following day, the same chief had a change of heart without explanation. He entered our village and warned everyone, including my grandfather and my eldest uncle, not to send my uncle away. Thus,

---

1   If someone leaves Hinduism, they lose whatever status they have in the caste system. Their status becomes lower than the lowest caste. They become "untouchable."

my Christian uncle was able to stay in the village and serve the people anyway.

We had no electricity, no driveable road, and no schools in our village. Fifty years later, there still isn't any road or any electricity in the area, but at least there are some primary and middle schools now. The area is very isolated in the high hills at the base of Mount Everest.

Though my uncle wasn't a well-educated man, he used to bring medicine from the city of Kathmandu, which was a very long journey: first a three-day walk to the bus station, and then a multi-hour bus ride. He literally washed the wounds of the people of our area, just as the Samaritan did in the parable Jesus told. Slowly people realized that my uncle was a good man serving the people with all his heart. He loved everyone and shared the Gospel with the love of Christ with them, but very few came to believe in the Lord. After many years, seven people had been baptized in a river.

MY CONVERSION

My uncle had given me and my father a small book called *The Way of Salvation*, which I read with an open heart. I could barely read, but my father had taught me the basics using a slate and chalk. As I read, it seemed as though someone was talking to me. I told my uncle about this strange experience, and he said the Lord *was* talking to me through the scripture in this booklet. I was very curious, and in order to learn more, I would sneak to my uncle's home at night so others wouldn't know. There were usually no people except my uncle and aunt in that dark room, having a service with their family. Because we didn't have candles, we used to light the kerosene lamp to read his Bible before they prayed.

When my own half-brothers from my father's first marriage and other relatives saw me going to my uncle's home, they began to reject me. I had become an untouchable.

For example, my step-grandmother wouldn't allow me to touch her water pot. In the village, we only had one water source. One time when I happened to touch her water pot, she became very angry with me, and immediately poured the water out on the ground and washed the pot.

I felt a great lack of peace as I read. My uncle explained that sin is the thing that gives us that uncomfortable feeling, but Jesus wants us to come to Him and repent.

I asked, "What does 'repent' mean?" God was convicting me of my sins, and I realized in my heart that I needed to change direction and ask forgiveness. I didn't know how to pray about these things, so I listened to my uncle's prayer of forgiveness and repeated his words. And so the Lord found me there.

Suddenly I had a desire to go many places and tell my friends about the change that happened to me. So I think my call actually goes back to that response to the Lord and the desire He immediately gave me. I did not get baptized right away.

MY FATHER'S CONVERSION

In the meantime, my father was studying the Bible, sitting under a tree every day and comparing it with all his Hindu religious books, namely the Ramayana, Mahabharata, Vedas, and the Gita. It took three full years for him to be convicted that Jesus Christ was the only way for him get to heaven and that he needed to repent. After my father came to believe in the Lord Jesus Christ, a big problem presented itself. The whole community stood against us. My father, who had been greatly respected in our society, now became the most rejected person.

The following month, my father decided to be baptized. My uncle was not a pastor, so they took the long walk to the bus to go to Kathmandu to find a pastor to baptize him, even though my father had to use his crutch.

Due to persecution, however, no pastor had the courage to do it. The government was sure to apply the rules aggressively if they learned anyone had baptized him: the constitution decreed that any person who baptized would be put in prison for six years. And so their threats held believers back, especially since my father had been a Hindu priest.

When no one in Nepal would baptize my father, my uncle took him on the long drive south to Raxaul in Bihar, India. There was a church called the Rauxmul Christian Church. The pastor was Pushpa Ranjan M., who agreed to baptize him in public. One old couple from the priestly Brahmin family (high caste) was watching my father in this service. As they listened to his testimony, they realized that there must be truth in Jesus if this man had travelled many days to another country just to receive baptism. They considered this sincerely, and accepted the Lord sometime later. And so my father and uncle returned from the trip after some ten to fifteen days.

THE NEW TESTAMENT: HIS BEST FRIEND

In Philemon's village, life went on as everyone helped each other when they worked in the field. But they refused to come to help Philemon and his father because they were considered untouchable, especially after his father's baptism. They did not want them in their homes, nor would they go into Philemon's house. Even if some came to help, they might refuse to eat the food that was cooked for them. It was not culturally acceptable to ask someone to work for you when they wouldn't eat the food that you gave them. So it became very hard for his family to live in the village. Philemon was still a small boy, so he did not understand all that was happening, but he knew that something was going wrong in his village.

As a shepherd boy, Philemon used to go with the cattle, goats and other animals into the forest. It was there he studied his New Testament. The New Testament became his closest friend. He remembers reading his New Testament while eating his food. It became very dear to him, and he cherished these times.

Because there was no school in their village, Philemon's father had taught him to read and write. In those days, children would use a slate board with soapstone (*khara dhunga*) to learn the Nepali alphabet.

One morning Philemon was weeping bitterly. His father asked him why he was crying, but he could not explain why. The answer was that he had a deep desire to study, and there was no school in his hometown and surroundings. In spite of this, he began preaching immediately after his conversion by handing out tracts and explaining the basics of the Gospel. The following year, his father and uncle talked about taking him to Kathmandu for school. But Philemon did not understand where his uncle was taking him.

PART TWO: BACKGROUND TO PHILEMON'S STORY

PREM PRADHAN'S STORY[2]

Like the rest of his countrymen in the Hindu kingdom of Nepal, Prem Pradhan had grown up as a Hindu. While serving in the British army during World War II, Prem heard the Gospel from one of Bakht Singh's[3] street teams in Darjeeling in West Bengal (in neighbouring India), and received Jesus as his Saviour there.

After Prem had learned more about being a Christian, the Lord called him to go back to Nepal and preach the Gospel to the millions there who had never heard the name of Jesus.

Prem soon resigned from his army commission, went to a Bible college in India for some theological undergirding, and then

---

2   Much of this section comes from *Historical Sketch of Prem Pradhan* by Doug Hsu, as told to Brother David from Engage Today. A longer version of Prem's story can be found in appendix one.

3   There are still connections to Bakht Singh's ongoing ministry, including literature and work. Even in Nepal presently, the Singh organization's missionaries are starting churches. In the WWII era, Bakht Singh preached all across India. He had gone to Britain to study engineering, and then went for a master's degree to Winnipeg in Canada. There in 1929 he met John Hayward, a Christian who gave him a New Testament. John and his wife Edith invited him to their house for Christmas. Bakht Singh went back to India a changed man, and became a national evangelist and church planter, spreading this new message across the nations and even ministering in other continents until 2000. After a time of fasting and prayer the Lord led him and his coworkers to establish local churches on the basis of Acts 2:42. It was this man's preaching teams that Prem heard in India.

went back to Nepal to evangelize. When the work increased in Nepal, he started sending his converted students to different Bible schools to prepare for service when they felt called to this. A large number of them went to a Bible college in the northwest run by Brother Paul (deceased in early 2018).[4]

Despite stiff government penalties for evangelism, Prem fearlessly proclaimed the Gospel in his homeland. In time, many people responded to his message and were baptized. But Prem paid a steep price—he was soon arrested and sentenced to six years in prison for evangelizing and baptizing. He had been baptizing eight people in Palpa and was caught at the scene.

In those days, Nepali prisons were literally dungeons of death—twenty-five or thirty bodies jammed into a tiny room without any ventilation or bathroom facilities. New inmates often passed out from the horrific stench within minutes of arrival. Prisoners slept on a dirt floor that crawled with rats, cockroaches, and lice. They were each allotted just one cup of cooked rice per day, and as a result, most of them became severely ill from malnutrition.

Prem's spirit withered after seeing these conditions. If the Lord had indeed called him to win souls and to plant churches, then why had He let him come here just to rot to death? But the Lord spoke to him, "I did call you to build my church, and you

---

4 Philemon's current assistant, Pratima, was one of the students who attended this Bible college. The college was run by an interdenominational mission established by Brother Paul. Philemon was the first Nepali student in that college, but had gone on his own. He was given a very respected place at the 2017 conference as alumni. Paul's sons took time to get to know Philemon. Elishiba and Pratima attended as well, as Philemon was given honours. The student body has grown from forty-five, when Philemon went there, to over six hundred students now. Their compound has many buildings. Paul was also a lawyer, and wrote many books. He lived in Delhi District and ran the Bible college next door in Haryana State.

will do it in here also." After the revelation, Prem began actively sharing the Gospel with his fellow inmates. Many put their trust in the Lord, and after being released many of them went out as evangelists throughout Nepal.

As time passed and the prison authorities saw that the oppressive conditions did not seem to dent Prem's evangelistic fervour, they decided to try breaking his spirit another way. They chained him hand and foot and threw him into the prison morgue, where the bodies of dead prisoners were kept. The authorities predicted that Prem would last only a few days in there.

The space was so small that he could neither stand up nor stretch out. In the darkness he could barely make out the shadowy outlines of the corpses, which were oozing foul-smelling

This picture of Brother Prem hangs in the multipurpose building used for teaching by Philemon's ministry (provided courtesy of Philemon)

fluids onto the floor beneath his shivering body. Unable to bear his circumstances any longer, Prem begged the Lord to take him home quickly. But again the Lord spoke to him, "I suffered so much for you. Are you not willing to suffer a little for Me?" At this, Prem's heart became lighter, and he began spending his days praising the Lord.

One day the guard overheard Prem and asked him to whom he was talking. Prem answered, "Jesus." Shining the flashlight into the darkness but not seeing anyone, the guard asked Prem where this Jesus was hiding. Prem then shared the Gospel with him, and the guard also became a believer.

When the prison authorities realized that Prem was leading one person after another to the Lord, they transferred him to another prison. But there he also refused to stop evangelizing, so they had to transfer him to still another prison. He was released after four and a half years of his first prison term, because it was the practice to release some prisoners on the king's birthday, and his turn had come up.

Altogether between 1960 and 1975, Prem spent a total of ten years in fourteen different prisons suffering for Christ. As a result of his witnessing, many in Nepal have become believers in Jesus.

PART THREE:
PHILEMON'S PREPARATION FOR SERVICE

BROUGHT TO BROTHER PREM'S SCHOOL, 1968-69

Philemon had never seen any motor vehicles in his life. After walking three days, he arrived with his uncle at a place where he could see some cars and trucks going by. When he asked what they were, his uncle told him, "The buses and the trucks are the mother and father and the small cars are their children," and

Philemon believed him. From this town and bus stop, they continued several hours on bus into Kathmandu, where there were so many other things he had never seen in his home village.

At the end of the third day, they arrived at brother Prem's rented house in Kathmandu. His uncle stayed with him until the following day, and on the third day he left for home, leaving Philemon alone with Prem. Since Prem was still a stranger to Philemon, he felt very lonely and wept very bitterly with his face towards the wall. His only hope was in the Lord. He used to pray while hiding himself in the quilt. He learned to pray about everything. When he did not have slippers for his feet, he prayed for some and the Lord provided slippers for him.

A few days after his arrival in Kathmandu, Philemon was given the job of carrying the firewood from Brother Prem's newly bought field to his rented house. Prem was planning to build his new school on the new property. Philemon also planted some fruit trees there and watered them as they began to develop the land. He wasn't thinking too much of the long term results, but when he visited more than thirty-five years later, some of these trees were still bearing fruit!

SCHOOL DAYS BEGIN

Philemon had never gone to any school until he was about thirteen years old, when he was admitted into third grade at Prem's new school. It was because of his home training that he was given the equivalent of grade three when he began at a real school. There were no chairs and benches in their school; therefore, students studied sitting on the bricks that were being stored while the school was under construction. God gave Philemon favour in the sight of the staff, and he became a monitor in the school and a leader in the hostel. He spoke Nepali, but here he was introduced to the English alphabet and English language, which would be useful in the future.[5] Philemon's name had been Krishna up until this time, a name given by a Hindu priest. Since that is the name of a Hindu god, his pastor suggested a change of name. Philemon thought about that for a while and then chose Philemon from the New Testament names he had read about.

BEING FILLED BY THE SPIRIT IN PREPARATION FOR SERVICE

Philemon had a burden to share the Gospel when he was first converted. He did not know anything about the Holy Spirit, since there had been no teaching about Him yet. But the Holy Spirit was already using him at this time.

Then a visiting Indian pastor and his wife taught about the Holy Spirit during the devotional class at the hostel at Prem's school. They also prayed for the sixty students. Philemon was

---

5 From *ANM* newsletter article "Prem Pradhan 1924–1998" (published 2017): "Probably the greatest work Prem did was to start schools for the training of young people. The first school he started was in Lazimpat, a section of Kathmandu. With funds sent by Christian Aid, Prem built a three-story building, gathered a teaching staff, and started teaching up to 250 children. From the top floor, one could look into the back yard of the king's palace. ...Without warning, in 1972 police raided the school, killed one teacher, and beat the others. Prem was imprisoned; the teachers fled; the children were scattered. Prem's sentence was for 20,000 days – 54 years (Bob Finley was responsible for raising $2000 for a ransom fine to allow him to leave jail)... In 1980 Prem began another school—this time on his farm in Sarlai District, a day's journey by bus from Kathmandu. ...By 1984, 1000 pupils were enrolled in New Life School. Most walk miles from the surrounding areas.
About 300 are children brought to Prem's farm from the mountains where there are no schools. They stay in boys' and girls' hostels built with funds provided by Christian Aid so they can attend Prem's school. ...In 1986 the King of Nepal awarded Prem the Social Service Medal of Honor for his humanitarian and educational work – perhaps as an act of atonement for the 1972 persecution."

very curious about the Holy Spirit, and wanted to be filled. He began to understand from the Bible and the pastor's teaching that a relationship with the Holy Spirit was part of the preparation for service.

On the next school holiday, he went home. While he was thanking the Lord for safe travel, he found himself not in his body but somewhere in the Spirit thanking the Lord. Philemon felt somewhat like the Samaritan and Ephesian believers in Acts who had an incomplete knowledge of the gift of salvation, which includes the sealing of the Holy Spirit, and therefore had an incomplete baptism.[6] Anyway, Philemon went back to school knowing he could count on the Holy Spirit's help in witnessing. He began to experience the Lord filling him, and he continued witnessing for the Lord.

But Philemon still didn't feel able to pray as he wanted to. He felt he needed to be broken in spirit. This was not something possible through his own effort, so he poured out his heart to the Lord.

Sometime later on a Saturday he was fasting and praying with his friends in a small house not very far from the school hostel. Without realizing fully what was happening, the Holy Spirit so convicted him that for several hours he did not know where he was. But to his surprise, when he opened his eyes he was still crying and praising God with tears running down his face. Philemon found himself a completely changed person. The burden on him was lifted; he felt the forgiveness of the Lord. The blood of Jesus Christ had indeed washed him and the old was gone. He became a newborn baby in the Spirit. He rejoiced and wanted to jump and dance for the Lord. He went to his friends back in the hostel and asked for forgiveness. Philemon felt just like a flower, very

---

6 Samaria: Acts 8:14–17; Ephesus: Acts 18:24–19:5

light. Very shortly after this Philemon was baptized by brother Prem in the river of Bishnumati in Kathmandu.

As he thought about the burden in his heart for the lost, he decided to go to remote villages with the Gospel. During the following winter at the time of public school holidays, Philemon went to the villages on foot to preach the Gospel. He witnessed about the Lord to whomever he met on the way—to his friends, relatives, teachers, and others.

At the same time, there was much persecution of the Christians in the area. The students had been actively singing and practicing their newfound Christianity at school. But the government had sent spies and in turn had warned and threatened the teachers about allowing these Christian activities. So the school authorities decided to forbid them to sing songs or pray in their school devotions because of the fear of persecution. Even some of the teachers were spying for the government. The risk was that someone would report to the government that the Christians were converting people to Christianity at the school. But Philemon was a new believer,[7] and was very excited to worship and pray and sing loudly to the Lord. In this situation he felt like a dying fish out of water. How could he not read and sing to God out loud as he deeply yearned to do?

Philemon asked the Lord what he should do in these circumstances. The Lord spoke to him from the book of Proverbs, saying that he would have to leave the place, and He would not allow his foot to stumble. Jesus Himself would guide him. When

7 There seemed to be only twenty-six or twenty-seven Christians in that area of Nepal when Philemon came to Christ. While there was little to no Bible teaching in the other areas, Prem taught a lot of Bible lessons at the hostel. Part of his strategy was to send his newly converted students to study in different Bible colleges outside the country—to Labat, Hordwar near Lucknow, and Uttar Pradesh—and when they came back, they taught the new converts and believers in Nepal.

he received this word from the Lord, he thought he would go back to his hometown in order to worship the Lord better—in the jungles, he could sing and pray as loud as he wished to. But before he could act on this, the pastoral couple from India invited him to come with them.

INVITED TO INDIA

At this time, in 1971, in his mid-teens, Philemon traveled with that same couple to Darjeeling. They had invited Philemon to be in their group called "The Lord's Army." He joined them and went along to this unknown area. They reached the state of West Bengal and took a train, arriving at 9:00 p.m. There was no vehicle for them to use when they arrived at the railway station, so they slept on the platform because it was rainy season.

The next day, the couple took him to a small mission compound where they stayed for three months. They preached the Gospel zealously, going to different towns and tea gardens around Darjeeling. Besides speaking, they also gave away many books. The Lord blessed the ministry, but they had a very hard time because there was no proper place to stay and no proper food to eat. The couple did not have a home either. Three big boxes and two bundles of bedding were everything they had. They used to carry those boxes and their three children wherever they went. Sometimes they did not have any food to eat, so the children and Philemon suffered with the parents. One time when there was nothing to eat, they boiled little flowers in water with some vegetables and ate this soup.

How little money they had is shown by this memory. Milk at that time was very cheap: just 40 paisa[8] per litre. Philemon had a great desire to drink some milk, but he did not have even 10 paisa

8 Like cents to dollars, there are one hundred paisa per rupee.

(the price of a very small cup of tea) to buy a quarter litre of milk, so he could not fulfill this desire. But in spite of the poverty, he spent a year with this wonderful mentor couple, witnessing about his Lord.

GRADE SCHOOL CONTINUES

Philemon had an opportunity to study through one of the orphanages of World Missionary Evangelism (WME)—Douglas Memorial Children's Home in Darjeeling, India. David, the pastor who started it, came with a camera one day and told Philemon that if he wanted to study more in a school, he would try to enroll him. After several months David came back and said, "You can go to this school and stay in the orphan home there." David had a connection with John E. Douglas from Texas and started five children's homes with his support, three in Darjeeling and two in Nepal.

So Philemon went along with Pastor David, who also had a vision for the poor and unreached. He stayed there for about a year (1972–73), but even after a few months, he found that most of his school friends were non-Christians and some were very worldly. He thought to himself that if he continued to be with them, instead of going to heaven he would go to hell. He did remain connected with Pastor David and the ministry of WME for more than twelve years, although he left the school after one year.

David at this time had a great vision for preaching the Gospel to lost souls, especially among the Nepali people. He was young and was energetic, going from village to village to plant churches in 1972 when Philemon met him. David mentored Philemon in the ministry and gave him a chance to work with him. He took him along on trips to Manipur, Assam, Arunachal Pradesh, Bihar, and West Bengal. David eventually oversaw over fifty evangelists covering Bihar, West Bengal, and Nagaland, and operated a school there as well.

When people began to persecute David as he went to these farther places, he was not affected, much like Jesus was able to answer the Pharisees. As a result, they decided to leave him alone. David was responsible for many going to Bible school in Nagaland and south India, which has resulted in many preaching the Word today. His encouragement has meant so much to many, including Rev. Dan Singh and others who are now working with Philemon.[9]

Philemon believed that the Lord Jesus Christ was going to come very soon, and thought that if he didn't help people get saved, he would have no reward from God. Therefore, he was anxious to go to Bible school right away and prepare himself for His service instead of staying to finish regular school. But there was no one to help him to go to Bible school. He went to Pastor David one night and asked permission from him to go to Bible school. His pastor told him to continue his secular studies until tenth grade as Philemon was only in seventh grade at that time. He spent several hours, even past midnight, trying to convince him. While it was good advice, Philemon was not satisfied with this answer and he told Pastor David he would go to Bible school anyway, so the pastor gave permission.

In 1973 Philemon decided to go to North India Bible Institute in what is now Hordoi, U.P., about 40 km from Lucknow, India. He had some friends in the area, but he did not know any details about the Bible school. After travelling three days by train, he was told that there was no spot available for him in the school. After his humble request, the principal said, "Let us wait and see if some students do not turn up; then you may have a chance

---

9   David's sons are all in the ministry and have a quality music band called Mercy; his wife is also a minister, and his daughters are in Canada presently.

to stay and study." By God's grace one person did not show up. Finally the Lord had opened the door for him study the Bible!

Philemon studied a year and then Pastor David said, "You already know how to preach, so you can come and do it." But Philemon knew that year had only taught him the basics, so he went back and completed the other years for his degree. He completed the course in 1976 at age twenty-one.

After completing Bible school, he preached the Word with greater zeal. Having no place of his own, he went back to Darjeeling and stayed at Pastor David's home, since they allowed him to use their dining room table as a bed and allowed him to eat with them. He went to night school during this time and completed grade ten while preaching during the daytime. This was the beginning of the twelve years of co-ministry that followed—and a bed is a bed!

During some of this time he received 101 rupees plus fifty paisa of monthly support from the pastor. Later the pastor found a church that would sponsor him at five hundred rupees per month, but fifty rupees were withheld for a tithe. During the latter years he also taught in the World Missionary Evangelism Bible School and preached in the tea gardens in the morning and evenings.

PART FOUR:
PHILEMON'S MINISTRY IN DARJEELING DISTRICT

NO OXYGEN LEFT

After about ten years of ministry, when Philemon's father became seriously ill, his eldest brother Bahadur brought him to Philemon to care for him. Now he had to rent at least one room for his father. At that time, he received about $9.00 per month—not even enough for pocket money. But he rented a single room which became their bedroom, kitchen, and living room.

One afternoon it was snowing and very cold outside, so they closed the door and the windows. They used charcoal to cook the food for their evening meal. As soon as Philemon finished cooking, he became sleepy, almost to the point of being unconscious, because little oxygen was left in the room. Somehow he managed to open the windows. They were too sick to eat the food that night. If the window had not been opened just in time, carbon monoxide poisoning would have killed them, but the Lord helped them to stay alive.

Philemon and his father later moved into another house which had just one room and one very small kitchen. When his Uncle Jagat and his other family members also came to stay there, it became very congested.

Now Philemon had to find a room for just his father and himself again! He started praying about this, and one of the church members who had only a small home in a tea garden, but a great heart, told Philemon that he would give a small single room to the two men. They stayed there for eight years.

MARRIED

Philemon had been praying for a life partner during this time—someone who feared the Lord like he did. On one of his tours to the hills of Darjeeling, he had a very successful Gospel crusade in a nearby town. Later he met a young woman, Elishiba, in another open-air Gospel meeting. This woman from that first town was singing Gospel songs which were blessing many people in a special way, as the Spirit seemed to have an anointing on her.

Elishiba was not thinking ahead to marriage while she was participating in the choir group—she was still in high school. But during her studies in Bible school, she began thinking that her husband would need to be a man of God. That would be good, whatever else might happen. She says, "I used to feel that whatever the trouble or challenge, I would be happy if my husband feared the Lord."

It seems there was some talk between them as they served in the same evangelistic events. However, Philemon's economic situation was so bad that he had only one pair of pants—he had to wear a towel while he washed and dried those at night. He had no expectation or hope of romantic interest due to his poor state. So he was afraid of talking with her father, but somehow her father understood the situation and told Philemon that he was okay with Philemon marrying Elishiba. Slowly the Lord brought them closer to each other, and they got married on December 20, 1985.

After the wedding, Philemon had to move to yet another room, which again felt no bigger than a closet. He was still serving the Lord without receiving a proper salary, still only receiving five hundred Indian rupees per month in support from his pastor. Elishiba took things in her stride; she says today, "Whatever the situation, I was happy with marriage from the beginning."

God gave Philemon much fruit in the form of precious souls and love from the people in the area. The church people asked for him more than the other preachers for their service in the villages, in tea gardens, and in other towns. That made his pastor jealous of Philemon, and he started putting him down.

SUPPORT STOPPED

The support Philemon had received from Nagaland Missionary Movement (through his pastor David) was stopped shortly after his marriage. Only a month later, he received a letter from the secretary of that organization, Reverend Ellis, saying, "Now the church that supports you has decided to discontinue your support as of January, 1986. I will be sending proper papers to you." They had somehow been told he was not in the area he had been assigned to. But even today everyone in those areas can tell you that Philemon was ministering there.

He never received the papers, but the great God who called him for His ministry remained faithful to him and taught him to trust in Him and Him alone. Praise God for His goodness.

"PEACELESS" OVER NOT SERVING THE LORD FULL TIME

A few months later, Philemon felt that he had to find a job. The Lord provided one for him in one of the Christian social services. The first question he asked his bosses was, "Can I witness for Christ during my break times?" They said yes, he could. But it did not work out that way and he was not able to witness on the job.

PhilemonH worked there with his whole heart for seven months, but he felt no peace. His family was able to have food to eat as the Lord provided, but he felt that his spiritual stomach was empty. His physical belly was full, but his spirit was starving, not because he did not have any spiritual fellowship, but because he did not have any opportunities to serve the Lord according to his calling.

THREE YEARS' LABOUR, ONE SINGLE SOUL

Finally after seven months, Philemon decided to resign his job to serve the Lord full time. One church called him to be their pastor. He served that small congregation of just three families for three years. They would give him five hundred rupees per month, so he finally had a salary again. It took him over a year to be able to afford to buy a new sari (dress) for his wife after they were married. So she wore the same sari for more than a year. But they continued to serve the Lord joyfully, Elishiba alongside her husband.

During those three years at Mungpoo, the Lord gave him one single person, Chitra,[10] who was saved and baptized. Chitra is now pastor of a church and also headmaster of a government school; he is married to Sarita, and parent to a teenage daughter (16) and son (15).

Chitra was a smart student, and he read extensively in many fields. He was reading a lot about demon worship and black magic at the time he met Philemon. Philemon would share about the Gospel, and encourage Chitra to read the Bible.

While Chitra's parents were Hindus, he knew something of Christian thought from some relatives who were Christians. He was quick to challenge Philemon's claims about Jesus, but Philemon would only say "Let's pray about it" in answer to any objections. Slowly, as Philemon kept introducing the Gospel, Chitra began to consider whether Christ was real. As a worshipper of many gods, he added Jesus to their number. These discussions went on for much of the three years.

But the Holy Spirit continued to draw Chitra to Himself, and he became the fruit that eventually grew into a church. This was in spite of immediate rejection by his brothers.

During this time Elishiba ministered with Philemon as she was able. People liked Elishiba's voice in church or choir, so she sang anywhere she was asked to in these years. In 1986 she went to Delhi, where a Christian worker they knew had a radio program with messages about grace. He had asked her, her brother Paul, and her sister to sing for the program. So some songs were

---

10 For the rest of the story and the testimonies of church members currently ministering along with Chitra, see appendix two.

recorded in a very good studio and later produced on cassettes which were distributed widely. This was a time when few Christian songs were available in Nepal, so the recordings were very helpful in India and Nepal for Nepali speakers.

Philemon worked as a pastor day and night, distributing many Bibles and thinking that the Lord would give him many more souls. But God had another plan for him. When he acknowledged that the Lord was not making him fruitful in the area, he started praying, asking the Lord to let him know His perfect will, even if he had to go through many kinds of hardships in the ministry.

During this time, God gave Philemon and Elishiba a family—a son, Samuel, and then another, Joel. After the boys were born, Philemon would sometimes go away on evangelism trips. It was hard for Elishiba if the boys got sick, as there was no money to take them to the hospital. They sometimes got sick just after he left, and then in turns. The house was rented, and it seemed the spirit of the idol-worshipping owners might have been involved with this situation. But later the couple would often take the boys along with them to meetings and to visit people, and Elishiba was happy to be involved.

Elishiba remembers that they only had a regular pot until finally a pressure cooker was purchased after Samuel was born. This may not seem so important, but black dal lentils take forever to soften without pressure, even with pre-soaking and boiling. So this was a great help to Elishiba after years of doing without.

Lentils as sold by the road today, including black lentils

Survival was sometimes the bottom line; there were times when they didn't know where the next meal was coming from, but it always arrived. This was made emotionally harder in Mungpoo, a place where they had a one-room home with a little kitchen outside. The neighbour would come when Philemon was gone and ask why they didn't have any land or their own home and other unnecessarily troubling questions. Philemon's answer to all these situations on his return was, "God will supply."

One day a man of God with the gift of knowledge spoke to Philemon, saying that he should leave that particular place and go to another. Philemon prayed for confirmation and decided to leave that village and go the place where the Lord would lead him. During that time the Lord called his father home to be with Him. After his father's funeral service on February 1, 1991, Philemon and his family moved to Darjeeling.

That year Philemon tried to get Samuel, his eldest son, admitted into one of the schools in Darjeeling. He tried three times, but could not get any placement for him in the schools. At that time he did not know why this was so, but later Philemon realized that being in this town was not the will of God. He had another plan for him: planting a new church in another town.

The Lord led Philemon to minister among his own people, and despite the difficulties, he has been faithful to the task.

NEW CHURCH PLANT

The Lord put a strong burden in Philemon's heart to plant a new church in another town. Kurseong was a new place for him, though it was not too far from Darjeeling. Philemon did not know how to get started there, so he went to Brother Prem Pradhan to ask his advice about this. Prem said, "Brother, it is not easy to start a church in a new place." But the burden did not leave him.

Prem told Philemon, "This will be so difficult because you have to look after the people once they come. It's not easy. Come help administrate my school and have a good job!"

But Philemon replied, "Papa, the Lord wants me to do it. I have been doing this for a long time, so I know what is needed." Of course this process was not new for him—Philemon knew very well how hard it is to plant a new church in a virgin area. Accordingly, he also knew that it was not hard for the Lord to do it.

Philemon said, "My calling is to reach the unreached. I want to start a church here." This seemed to be part of his burden from the Lord. He didn't have any believers there, but the Lord kept saying, "Go start a church." So they left Darjeeling the following year and started the church with seven people, including his two little boys, Samuel and Joel. Philemon prayed and asked the Lord for more souls.

Since Prem was starting another school nearby in this city, Philemon asked him if he could use one dark damp room. Prem agreed, and Philemon laid down the one woolen carpet he had so people would have something to sit on. This carpet was inherited from his father, and had come with his father from Nepal.

On March 8, 1992, he started the church. (He served the Lord for three years there.) He again went out preaching the Word of the Lord. Philemon didn't know how the church plant would start, but one of the men who had heard him speak came and asked, "Pastor, do you have a Bible?" So Philemon gave him one and the man left.

Then Philemon had a dream: on his right side, there was a rice paddy, fully ripe and ready to harvest. The next day, he went to find the man to whom he had given the Bible, and found his house was in an area right beside a ripe paddy, filled like in the dream! The man started studying with Philemon, and that became the beginning of the church.

DEALING WITH DEMONS

Although the man wanted to know the Bible, his home was not hospitable because his wife was a witch doctor. The next time Philemon's team visited the area, the man came to ask for prayer for his wife, so Philemon and several others went late in the evening to the house to pray. The wife was at the meeting, and demons manifested. So for many hours until dawn, they prayed for her and finally cast the demons out from her as the strength of Christ was displayed. When they finished, the man said, "We will now believe in the Lord." He took out all of the gowns that she used for enchantments, and they made a fire and burned them.

Philemon often went to visit people from home to home. Then when some of them became new believers and came to meetings, they brought friends who were prayed for. Most of them asked to be delivered from Satan's demonic power, while some asked for healing. Many healings followed. When these people had their prayers answered, the truth of Philemon's teaching had more credibility and the congregants became more involved in witnessing. Within two years, there were almost two hundred newcomers attending the church.

One day Saayan, one of the staff in Brother Prem's school, also asked Philemon for a Bible. He was a devoted Hindu. Although Saayan started attending church, Saayan's wife was still a witch doctor being used by the devil. She had many disciples among the Hindus.

One of Saayan's daughters, Sushma, who was studying in the college, became seriously sick and they took her to the hospital.

After some treatments, the doctors sent her home to her parents because they were not seeing any improvement in her symptoms. The sickness was not a physical one—she was possessed by demons. She became more seriously ill in her parent's home, and at this time they asked Philemon and Elishiba to pray for her. The Lord Himself miraculously delivered her. Then Saayan's whole family started coming to the church.

Because Sushma's mother had been a witch doctor, it was truly hard for her to follow the Lord. While prayers were made to cast the demon out of her, it would say from within her, "I will not leave you!" But the Lord delivered her with His resurrection power, and did convict her. She gave up everything of the devil that had been part of her life as witch doctor. Philemon still remembers the day when Sushma's father burned his wife's long gown, which she used to wear during the rituals of devil worship. The whole family decided to take water baptism together. But a strange thing happened on the day of their baptism.

A STRANGE THING HAPPENED

On the day of their baptism, Sushma's mother became blind and said to the rest of the family members, "I will not go for baptism because I can't see to walk to the baptism tank." The other family members said that they would carry her. Philemon was not told about what had happened to her.

Philemon baptized all the people who were ready for baptism, including Sushma's mother, who was blind. After the baptism service they told him that she had become blind before her baptism and was not able to see anything. But after she got out from the baptism tank, her eyes were opened and could see as before. Praise God! That was a great miracle, and she witnessed to other people about what the Lord had done in her life. Her family has been a great help to the church since that time.

Their daughter Sushma became seriously sick one afternoon after the church service. That Sunday, the church was observing the Lord's Supper. Just when everyone was beginning to go home, she was again possessed by the evil spirit. Brother Prem and Philemon and other brethren started casting out the evil spirit, and it said from within her that it would not leave her but would rather drink her blood. It took more than three hours to cast this demon out of her. Thank God, He delivered her, and since then she has been totally free.

The Lord did other miracles in the lives of the people, and the church continued growing. Elishiba and Philemon gave Bhibhu, a man of God, the responsibility of that church before they left for Kathmandu and the greater ministry God had prepared for them. And Sushma got married to Bhibhu! He ministered under Philemon for a time and became a supervisor, and is still serving the Lord in this same church, but is now associated with another Christian group.

In another incident in the same church during that time, there was a woman who was mentally disturbed. She had also returned from the government hospital. Her relatives called the church people to pray for her. Before Philemon went to pray, some of the other church members had arranged a prayer meeting for her in their house. Before he arrived at the prayer meeting that night, the youth were singing hymns.

When he came into the house, this lady, who had not even been able to get up from her bed, began acting like a predatory lion and came towards him. She wanted to grab him and harm him. She was kicking the stone wall next to her so strongly she almost broke it. It was rumbling, even though it was made of large stones. But Philemon stood there and said, "Do you know who I am? Stop in the name of the Lord!" When he said this, she fell back like a paralyzed person. After the singing was finished, Philemon preached the Word to the mixed group of people—Hindus, Buddhists and Christians. Finally they prayed for this sick woman. Philemon heard her belly, which was bubbling noticeably. He had never seen this type of scene before—the body was not moving at all except for the belly. After the prayer he told the family to let her rest and they went home.

The next day, Saturday, while Philemon was in town, someone visited his home. He asked who the visitors were. It was this woman and her husband. When he met them, he could hardly believe his eyes, because he had seen her taken to the bedroom with the help of two other women just the previous evening. But it was true—she and her husband were the couple that visited his home that day. They came to church the next day. Our God is great and does great miracles.

NOTHING COULD STOP HER FROM FOLLOWING THE LORD

There are many stories like this, but here is one more as an example. One night Philemon was leading a regular cottage meeting in one of the areas in the town, and a Christian from another church entered whom Philemon had never met before. He had come to take Philemon to pray for someone who was seriously sick.

After they finished the cottage meeting, they followed him to pray for this sick person, a young girl of eighteen years. They prayed for her, and the Lord had mercy on her and healed her. But her body had been so weak for so long that her stomach was not ready for her to digest much food at a time. Because her mother Meena allowed her to eat whatever she wanted, she became sick again and was hospitalized. After a few days, she died.

This girl had been the only daughter and future hope of Meena, whose husband had died while serving in the British army. Meena's father and one of her brothers had also passed away. There were three widows in the family including her. No one in the family was a Christian yet, but Meena decided to follow the Lord at any cost. She said, "Even though my only daughter has died, I will follow the Lord."

Philemon did not have any words to console Meena. The Lord gave him just one verse of the Bible that says, "...in all things God works for the good of those who love him" (Romans 8:28, NIV). He told her this time and again, and she believed the Word of God. The Lord God honoured her faith, and blessed her with great peace.

Later Meena asked for baptism, and Philemon baptized her along with other people. This experience showed that the Lord clearly had a special plan for her life. In a short period of time, the Lord saved many souls through her, including her widowed mother, the wife of one of her brothers, and her two fatherless nephews. In fact, among the more than two hundred people in this church, most have come to the Lord through the labour and witness of this widow named Meena.

GOD HAD A DIFFERENT PLAN

Philemon was completely settled in India and serving the Lord with his whole heart, as well as visiting Nepal from time to time for short-term ministry. But it was not the will of God for him to be in India his whole life and serve Him from there.

It was about this time that Brother Prem kept requesting Philemon to send someone from India to come and minister with him in Nepal. Philemon was comfortable in India, so he asked others to go. A few considered, but when they heard about all the government restrictions on Christianity in Nepal, they changed their minds.

CHRISTIAN LIFE WAS HARD

When Philemon was a child, Christians were seen as outcastes: excommunicated from their relatives and families, and kept from water sources. Philemon remembers, "As a young person, I was not questioned about the Bible I was carrying. But I was questioned once about reading my Bible in a hotel. The district officer questioned me fairly harshly about being a Christian, taking all of my particulars as if he would arrest me, but by God's grace he was transferred before he could carry out his plans."

Christians often had to hide, so in the area where Christianity began to spread in Nepal almost fifty years ago, they would spend their days in the caves, come out and preach in the evenings, and then disappear again. The government would send spies to find Christians and check on conversions, especially seeking evidence of baptismal ceremonies. In the 1960s there were only a handful, but this changed in the 70s and following, as those faithful few spread the Word whether in or out of jail.

DECISION TIME

After about three years of prayer, Philemon and Elishiba finally felt compelled to go back to Philemon's homeland. So they went to Kathmandu to minister alongside Prem in January, 1996. This ministry involved work not only in the capital itself, but also tribal work to the south and west of Kathmandu. The responsibility was to become much greater in 1998, but no one was aware of the changes that would come. Two students of Prem also played a part in the events of 1996–2000. Dhan had reached the status of teacher after going to Prem's school for years and then being sent for teacher training. Pratima became his wife during this time, and Philemon presided at their wedding. Survey trips with Dhan and his friend into the Chitwan and Makwinpur area also brought Philemon into contact with a man called Habil during this time. Dhan went on to work closely with Philemon for fourteen years, and Habil has been working as area supervisor in that district since that time.[11]

PART FIVE: PHILEMON'S MINISTRY IN NEPAL

STEPPING OUT BY FAITH

Like Abraham, Philemon left India by faith, not knowing what was going to happen in the future. He had his wife Elishiba and two sons, Samuel (9) and Joel (5). They had no future security, and no assurance from anyone. His prayer to the Lord was, "I don't mind trials, but I need to know Your will." He would face whatever came before him in serving the Lord.

Without any human authority over his new ministry, Philemon was serving the Lord by visiting churches in different areas that no one cared about. He was nobody to them. People thought he came from India to gain something; but his God, who called him for the ministry of the Kingdom, proved through miracle-working that He had sent him back to Nepal to serve Him in a greater way.

---

11 These events are chronicled later in Philemon's story.

Churches in Kathmandu and other parts of Nepal started growing fast, and every now and then there were baptisms.

One man from the US questioned Philemon in Kathmandu as to why he had come to settle there. Philemon said, "This is a capital city and from here you can go everywhere in Nepal. I want to go all over Nepal to reach the people of Nepal." The American kept pressing with the same question. Philemon simply replied, "To do the will of God." And then the man was satisfied. Philemon is still carrying out that ministry.

Brother Prem was already working with the Chepang people when Philemon started meeting them. Prem had used Dhan and another brother in his early work in this area, but had also involved Philemon earlier with seminars there and then again after he moved to Kathmandu. Habil came to the Lord through some of the converts of missionaries who were later connected with Prem's people. Philemon started working with Habil during this time, and nineteen churches came out of Prem's ministry there.

TRIALS

Satan could not tolerate the growth of the church. He stood against the church of the living God, trying to scatter the whole body of believers.

Brother Prem took Philemon to the USA to introduce him to his friends there in 1997. Satan had a good opportunity to destroy the church by dividing the Kathmandu congregation into two parts during their time away. He did it with the help of a man whom Brother Prem educated in his school and sent to be the replacement while Philemon was gone. This matter needed to be attended to upon their return, and this man was removed from ministry.

On Philemon's return, God continued to bless the ministry with many souls, and again the church grew. But Satan did not like it and tried another method, removing the congregation from the place in which they used to worship. On August 11, 1999, Philemon received a phone call at 9:30 p.m. saying, "After tomorrow, you are not going to use that place anymore for prayer meetings." The next day was Thursday, which was the prayer day for the church. That was also the day Philemon had to travel to India to perform a marriage ceremony. Overnight they had to vacate the place. Philemon requested that they be allowed to use the hall at least for the following Saturday service, but the official refused.

HE COULD HARDLY SLEEP THAT NIGHT

Early next morning, Philemon woke up and went to meet his congregation. He told them what had happened the previous night. They quickly understood the situation, and before noon that day they had vacated the compound. Thus, the place where they had worshipped the Lord for several years was closed permanently.

Philemon did not know where to go for the next worship service. One dear member broke down the middle wall in her house, and said they could hold the service there for some time. But the space was not enough to contain all the congregants. Therefore the congregation was divided into three groups that met separately for several months. In the meantime, the Lord God provided a piece of land (8 anas, or just over 250 square metres) to build the church, and Philemon paid Rs.1080000 (one million and eighty thousand rupees, equal to approximately $2100 CAD) including the government tax for the land; however, there were no finances to construct the church building.

THE FAITHFULNESS OF GOD SHOWN
IN THE CONSTRUCTION OF THE BUILDING

There was discussion over how to proceed. Two colleagues said a multipurpose building for the church was needed. Philemon ran here and there for loans.[12] He took a loan from one of his relatives and thought of constructing a meeting hall first. The government needed an access road to allow them to do any construction work, but there was none. Philemon had to purchase another piece of land to join the original property to the closest road. This property included space for a future access road as part of the agreement, as there was none next to the land. It was only after this that they were able to construct a meeting hall for God's people to gather for worship.

This hall was not much better in the beginning than a shed. There were only two small windows in the building, with a tin roof. Later they put in four more windows, an inside ceiling, electricity, and fans. Now, at least light could come into the hall. Later, the congregation added a sound system; it finally felt more like a place of worship, and is still in use today, almost two decades later. Praise the Lord! He provides.

The Lord, by His mercy, helped Philemon to gather some more money to purchase another piece of land adjoining this meeting hall. After much prayer, he started believing the Lord would supply a multi-purpose building to fulfill several functions, such as for a short-term Bible training school, or to have people to stay in while they came for conferences.

In 2000, Philemon traveled in the USA and shared this vision with various congregations. While visiting a church where he had friends, he received an envelope with $25; there was no indication of the giver, but it said "Bible School in Nepal." When

---

12 In Asia, loans often come from personal connections rather than banks.

he enquired about the source, someone told him they wanted to be anonymous. With this envelope he went to Pastor Eric, the mission pastor of the church, and asked him to bless the gift with his prayers.

With this money, Philemon came back to Nepal, and by faith asked two of his co-workers to start the work for the Bible school. They did the planning and got permission from the government, but there were no funds for construction. By faith, Philemon asked the contractor to carry out the work. They started building it slowly, piece by piece, starting with engineer's drawings and a hand-dug foundation, and later adding verandas and windows. After a few months he received $11,700 from Christ Community Church in the USA. That helped to increase his faith.

There was a time when Philemon had to ask the contractor to stop the work. But again the Lord helped provide some designated and undesignated funds. Philemon put the money into the Lord's hand, and Jesus blessed it just like the five loaves of bread and the two small fish. By the time they finished the multi-storey multipurpose building, they had spent nearly 3,700,000 rupees (approximately $70,000 Canadian at that time).[13]

This building is used in many ways, and it is great to fulfill hosting when groups visit, or when a seminar is being held on the adjoining lot. The multipurpose building has also been used to run a three-month training program as a Bible college, which has happened about once a year from 2003 until 2015. The building is

---

13 A total of $125–150,000 was spent over time on this property's buildings, including a three-story school and training building with a third story apartment/dorm, two separate smaller church and Sunday school buildings, a separate living quarters for a groundskeeper/watchman, and separate washrooms which are used when a large tent is raised for special meetings, like leadership seminars, with several hundred attending.

also used by other discipling groups, and is used now by Philemon for week-long training sessions of pastors and church workers.

God has also supplied a house for Philemon in the years following. This was a gift from friends—a sturdy house that is also an administrative centre, with guestrooms for supervisors and other visitors to stay with Philemon when they come.[14] The mission is run very frugally, on a faith basis, but this special gift and the public position given to Philemon by the TV opportunity have made him a high profile person who has had opportunity to meet and influence those in high positions. With this influence, he has encouraged political leaders to allow Christians to meet together to worship in a public way, and been able to reach people across the land with the Word.

WORKING FOR GOD CAN BE MESSY

Philemon had some unforgettable experiences during and after the construction. He only had two men working alongside him in the ministry in this church. The three of them were like one man when they worked together, laboured together, laughed together. That was why Philemon purchased the land jointly in three names, including his. He asked one of them to help him in the work of construction to purchase the materials, but sometimes Philemon also asked him to take someone else along to help him to buy the things and bring them back. Sometimes the man did so, but other times he did not like to take another person with him. Philemon did not know why, but later he found out that the

---

14 All the buildings mentioned in this section survived the last major earthquake, although a fair portion of the wall around the church needed to be rebuilt.

man thought that Philemon sending someone with him meant that he did not trust him.

When Philemon heard this, it was a shock. He asked his friend how this thought had come to him. Philemon said, "I only have one heart and one mind to think about anything, and I know even if I had one hundred hearts and hundreds of minds I would never have thought those things about you." In the long run, this man gave him lots of trouble in the ministry. Philemon could not even conduct the Bible school in 2004, because at that time if he had wanted to do some ministry on the property, this man would have interfered and created problems.

But here too, God answered through the prayers and suggestions of others, which helped him to overcome this problem. Praise God for this trial, because by the grace of God and the tearful prayers of others the matter was solved. The faithful core of the church remained, and continues to be strong.

There was a further matter of land exchange and another church started on that new land exchanged for this man's share, where the former partner is still working. The problem involved some followers who were more on the fringe—less committed and less discipled—and so that church has had its struggles with people leaving as well. But the Lord is still bringing in new believers, and the other man is learning how to deal with similar problems himself as he continues to minister today.

As Philemon thought back to this situation, he reported that the Lord is continuing to establish churches in both India and in

Nepal. The growth is faster than one would expect, and God is doing this in multiple ministries to reap a large harvest of souls.[15]

MEDIA MINISTRY BEGINS

Rather than Philemon, Elishiba was the one who started the media ministry. Even just after getting married, she was asked to record some Nepali songs for a Christian radio program in India, and these cassettes were duplicated and spread far and wide.

Sometime later, after Philemon became involved in radio and television, he wrote some songs with Elishiba's brother Paul, and Elishiba recorded these, both on CD and DVD, for use in his media ministry. They aren't sold, but are given away as a good tool for worship and discipleship. This is perhaps indicative of the pattern of their ministry, as Elishiba has been involved in outdoor meetings, singing, doing women's work, and even preaching whenever opportunities come her way.

In 2008 a man called to ask whether Philemon would be interested in being on the radio. This was something entirely new to New Life Ministries (NLM),[16] but Philemon said he would pray about it. Philemon and Elishiba prayed because they felt they had to know the Lord's leading, not just the need. Both

---

15 Since these events, Philemon has been in the US several times, and visited Canada in 2008 (with his wife), 2015, and now in 2019. Those churches are growing well, but most of the increase is in the southern area of the country. Those farther away in India and eastern Nepal are not multiplying as fast, although keeping count is difficult as sometimes these churches join with other groups once they mature. There were more than 160 churches as of March, 2018.

Some of the big changes have come with what seemed like government instability in Nepal. This actually meant that the pressure on Christians was reduced, and they have grown steadily for several decades. Recently the pressure has increased again with an updated anti-conversion law. There is more fear, and yet still the understanding to carry on regardless of obstacles.

16 This ministry was founded and run by Prem, and will be discussed later on.

came to see that God was leading them this way, and they started slowly with one station in 2008, not knowing whether it might last for one year—or even six months. There was a quick response for prayer, and gradual growth, with responses coming from many—communists and Hindus, students, politicians, and villagers. This pattern continues until today, as they receive good general comments from all strata of society in Nepal. Some of the stations have already celebrated a ten-year anniversary.

. In 2009, Philemon was asked to take a half hour on government TV on Sunday mornings (the equivalent of Monday mornings in North America) as part of an effort to improve representation of minorities in the country. The television program started in a similar way to the radio ministry—with a trial in 2009—and also received a good response, so he was asked to continue. There has only been one weekly program of twenty-five minutes allotted to the Christians, so it is a great privilege and responsibility.

Faith has been the funding method for both media since the beginning, and still is after more than a decade. Elishiba prays, which is perhaps the biggest way she is a backbone in the ministry, while Philemon works. They have maintained a production office where programs for both radio and TV can be produced. And so these tools are being used in effective ways to bring people to the Lord.

As Philemon looks at his ministry, preaching the Gospel and bringing the lost to Christ have always been the heart of the ministry's vision. Radio and television help to expand the Kingdom and reach and teach millions more than personal ministry can. They are able to reach spots that are very isolated in terms of physical accessibility. Media also covers all classes of society, including the prime minister, people that would not listen otherwise, and places Philemon can't reach or wouldn't be allowed to enter. Through this method, Philemon is in their living room or on their mobile phone. The TV program is also carried by internet to over one hundred countries where Nepali people have gone to find work. Once a Hindu politician introduced another religious leader to Philemon as if Philemon was someone he knew, and that was because he had often seen him on TV.

OTHER MINISTRIES

God has also allowed Philemon's ministry to have two schools in each country. In India, there is one with about thirty students for the Sherpa tribe (mountain guides), who asked Philemon to run a school for them, and another for the general tribal group in the northern tip of West Bengal, where there are presently twelve churches under his supervisors. Many other planted churches are ongoing, but have joined local ministry groups. In Nepal, one of the two schools is run for the Chepang children.

CHURCH PLANTING AND MENTORING

There is a lot of informal encouragement involved as well. When you are well known, people come to you with questions. Philemon reports,

> When people come to me to ask for help, I try to aid them in some way, or to connect them to others near them. At present, there are more people coming to me with their visions and needs than there are new workers going out to reach people.
>
> When someone new comes, we spend some time talking about God's leading. We try to bless those with

courage to start other works. Many new areas are very poor to begin with, and need encouragement, prayer and resources. And we ourselves are in a position of needing resources both for the media and for the church ministries.

Philemon has laboured for the Lord long and hard in his home country of Nepal. "From the time I began my ministry, the Lord Himself has been with me wherever I was," he says. "Praise God for His promises."

TRIBAL MINISTRY

Part of Philemon's ministry includes working with different tribes: Chepang, Tamang, Bhujel, Chhetri, Dalit, Brahmin and others. Some of his early work with Prem Pradhan involved weeks surveying a new area.

Six hours south and then five hours west of Kathmandu (or longer depending on construction timeouts) by solid vehicles on a winding road through the hills are two districts known as Chitwan and Makwanpur, which presently have forty-three development centres of about 4500 people in each. Municipalities in the area comprise about five of these centres each, which makes for about 20,000 in each one. Buses reach much of the area now, as there have been more roads built in the last few years.

PART SIX:
PHILEMON'S MINISTRY IN SOUTH CENTRAL NEPAL

THE CHEPANG[17]

Two accounts of the Chepang illustrate their situation when Philemon first went into the area.

---

17 Chepangs, believed to be influenced by Tamangs, speak their own distinct language, leading a nomadic life. Their primary lifestyle consists of hunting, foraging for wild roots, fishing, and traditional farming near jungles. (http://holidaymountaintreks.com/chitwan-chepang-culture-siraichuli-hill-trail.html).

According to Wikipedia, "Over the past two or three generations, the Chepang have begun to slowly shift from a semi-nomadic (slash-and-burn) lifestyle to a more settled way of life, relying increasingly upon the production of permanent fields of maize, millet and bananas. The severe topography, however, has made permanent farming difficult (and usually insufficient), and the forest has remained an important (although decreasingly so) source of food for the Chepang. Historically, the collection of wild yams and tubers, fish caught from nearby rivers, bats and wild birds, and periodically wild deer hunted from nearby forests, have supplemented their need for carbohydrates and protein. With increasing populations, lack of arable land and few irrigation options, malnutrition has been a historic problem for the Chepang despite forest supplements. The Chepang have often been characterized as the poorest of Nepal's poor." (Wikipedia. "Chepang People." Accessed September 10, 2018. https://en.wikipedia.org/wiki/Chepang_people)

NO REGULAR CLOTHES

Twenty-five to thirty years ago, the Chepang tribe lived in the jungle. At that time, they made their own clothing, but not anything like what we might have in the West. The government became aware of their existence when they were still living in caves and in the jungle, but by now most of them have come out from these places. Even after they came out, only the older people would wear something like a shirt or loin cloth—the children were naked while they were playing. If someone came to visit in their home, they would just go and grab some of their parents' clothes and put them on.

That was the circumstance when Philemon first met them. Some of the Chepang are still living in caves. They are good at making anything needed from the forest around them.

Woven carrying bag made of strands cut from forest materials; good for carrying anything from vegetables to books

The land where the Chepang live is not good for cultivation. They live in the mountains, and fertilizer doesn't stay on the sloped hills. In the rainy season, nutrients are washed away, so their local agricultural condition is poor, and therefore the economy is poor as well. The frequent shortage of food has several causes.

Even if the local people work hard, they will only have food for four to six months. The rest of the time, they have to go to the jungle to forage. They also hunt, but mainly they go searching for roots, which their people call yams. Everyone goes into the jungle for this purpose. Their area is now good for animal husbandry, but when they had just come out from the jungle, they did not have the knowledge to work with livestock.

THEY HAD NOT EATEN FOR THREE DAYS

One time when Philemon visited a village in this area, there were three children who were just crying and crying.

When he asked why, Pastor Habil told him, "They are crying because they have not eaten for three days."

"Where are their parents?" Philemon asked.

Habil told him, "I don't know where the mother is, but the father went to the jungle to find roots three days ago." While Philemon was talking with the children, their father came with a yam. He cleaned it, boiled it, and put some salt on it, and that is how he fed his children.

Another time when Philemon's team was travelling, they found some hungry children and gave them some of the flat rice they had brought along to feed themselves. The rice was what we would call rolled rice[18]—like rolled oats, a kind of local equivalent

---

18 Rolled rice is made up of oval flat flakes about 1.5 cm long, much like rolled oats but thinner.

of granola for wilderness trips. Because they had given some of this food to the children, they didn't have enough for themselves on the way back, so Habil and the others ate lemons they found on a tree nearby, just to have something in their stomach.

Children eating flat rice and beans during a conference with the Chepang

BRING YOUR OWN RICE

If you went to the Chepang as a guest, sometimes they wouldn't have any rice to give you. You would be wise to bring along rolled rice for yourself, or the hosts might borrow it from some other home. One time Philemon and others were visiting, and they bought one chicken for their hosts. They thought that the hosts would at least have rice to cook. But they didn't, so the host went to their neighbours and found some rice, and then gave it to the visitors for dinner.

The Chepang also found it hard to educate their children. They had difficulty in finding jobs because they were not educated. Philemon's answer for this was for the mission to start a school for the Chepang children. Some of their young people are now educated and can go out searching for a job—some of them are drivers for car owners in the town. So their economic situation is a little bit better now than a couple of decades ago, particularly as they now realize that their area is suitable for livestock and have learned how to take care of animals, and the resulting jobs have allowed some to gain further education.

HOW THE WORK EXPANDED
IN CHEPANG AND NEIGHBOURING AREAS

During the late nineties and early twentieth century, God expanded the ministry into a remote and unreached part of Nepal. This involved the work of several key associates, including Dhan and Habil.

DHAN'S STORY

Dhan has been a key member of both Prem and Philemon's work. "Project Philip" was a course started by a Bible society in India. Philemon took books from this group and distributed their new study to recent converts. Dhan's name was included in this list, and Dhan completed the course materials and sent them back. During this time, Dhan enrolled in Prem's school. He later finished tenth grade. While in college, Dhan started a church along the Bihar border.

Philemon got to know Dhan and his friend during this time, and when Philemon came to Kathmandu, they helped him find a place to stay. They also went on surveying and preaching trips to the Chepang area together from 1996–1998 as part of their work with Prem, who himself had also taken part in the earlier trips.

DHAN SPEAKS:
HIS TIME AT PREM'S SCHOOL AND MINISTRIES

In 1984, I had a month of Bible training in brother Prem's farm/home. I was baptized there. Then I joined his school and completed my high school in 1990. During my school days, I also had the responsibility of sharing the Gospel at the children's home run by Prem. Many young people accepted Christ.

I first visited Chepang villages about 1989. After a couple of years (1992/93), I, along with a friend, again visited the Chepang people's region for a survey (sent by brother Prem). During this trip, I first met brother Habil (about twenty-three years old at this time—two years older than me). He was probably not baptized at the time, but he had accepted Christ. He led us to one of the mountainous areas. He had a great zeal to share the Gospel with the people. I still remember one of his requests to me: he wanted to build a small worship house because Chepang people used to have just a one-room house. Whenever there were more than ten to fifteen believers, the room was not big enough to have a meeting. I was not in the position to help him at that time, so I just prayed with him for this need to be fulfilled soon. I visited seven major areas where the Chepang lived, and found some believers established in each place.

My longest trip was for two weeks. After getting off the bus from Kathmandu to Lothar (192 kilometers), I walked five hours with Habil on the same day to reach the nearest destination. It was close to rainy season, and rained very hard the whole night. We squeezed into a small hut. However, there was no rain in the morning. The next day was one of the longest parts of the journey. We walked eighteen hours that day. There was no house to host us. Finally, we reached a place at 11:50 p.m. where there was a believer's house. He was so glad to see us. I asked the believer not to prepare any meal for us because it was too late. But he prepared one anyway. After the meal, we prayed together before we went to sleep. It was already 2 a.m.! The next day, we continued our journey, visiting several places. On the way, we encouraged believers and leaders. We also supervised some worship house sites.

Dhan's future wife Pratima had also been placed in Prem's school as a young girl, after her father died and her mother could not afford her schooling. She was sent on to Bible school by brother Prem, who did this with many of his Christian students if they had an interest in serving the church.

Dhan was with Philemon when he went on his first evangelistic working trip for Prem. There was another man who often came with them for surveying, seminars, and building church halls. That work is continuing even today as they are still building churches, with many areas left to reach.

While Philemon was planting a church in Kathmandu, Dhan had already been on the teaching staff at Prem's secular school in another place since 1996. After completing his Bachelor's degree in education in a city called Birgunj (1997), Dhan worked as a high school teacher at Prem's school. Besides his teaching, he was still involved in planting churches with Brother Prem, which led to his desire to go to a theological seminary. But Prem wanted him in the position of the principal of the school (which Philemon had also passed up.) He was in the process of training to be the principal in 1998.

PREM'S DEATH BRINGS CHANGE

A relatively short time later, at the end of 1998, Prem died. It was a fairly sudden thing—he had a stroke and fell while taking a bath where he ministered, and was taken to a hospital in Raxaul, India, where he had another two strokes. The other leaders there planned to have an ambulance bring him to Kathmandu the next day, but he died before 8 p.m. on the same day. So Philemon had to go by bus to Sollai, about nine hours away, in order to conduct the funeral. They arrived after dark, and Philemon went to conduct the funeral on arrival since things were pretty much ready, including the burial place, and decay was an issue.

In his own ministry, Philemon was asked to absorb Prem's Nepali church-planting organization, known as New Life Mission (NLM), and add it to his own. So his leadership was confirmed. It was shortly after this time that Dhan requested to join Philemon in his work. Prem's work was divided after his death, with the Nepali church planting works given over to Philemon's leadership, and the secular schools in Nepal and India continuing under the leadership of Prem's son and family.

When Dhan called, Philemon said he could not promise a good salary like the school paid, but whatever Philemon had he would share with Dhan. So Dhan decided to come along with his wife Pratima. Philemon had officiated their marriage in Kathmandu, and they have since served with Philemon in many capacities for fourteen years. This has become part of the pattern. Those coming on board need to depend on God for support, and then Philemon will help them when possible as God supplies.

Dhan had been doing very good work, including much of the oversight of Philemon's Bible college. He was both registrar and one of the teachers. Dhan relates what a learning experience it was.

I have been involved in this Bible college since it first started. I have worked in different capacities: communicating with the church leaders to send the students, taking care of administrative work, and teaching various subjects. Sometimes, it was not an easy job to manage the students from different ethnic backgrounds. I tried my best to keep them in harmony and unity. I myself learned many things while serving there.

Philemon was thinking of developing him as the next leader. Dhan did everything: doing reports and accounts as office assistant, carrying out field visits in both India and Nepal, overseeing church building projects, and filling the role of one of the local church elders. Dhan went to Christ for the Nations for training as recommended and arranged by Philemon. He found ways to pay his own way, while Philemon supported Dhan's wife, father and mother-in-law, and three children.

Pratima worked in the office, where she is still involved part-time. There was no emailing system during that time, but telephone communication was actively used for receiving calls from listeners and answering them as well. She often sent letters and books to the listeners via the post office. Most of the time, people would request prayer for their problems, like sickness, depression, family issues, and so on. She would pray for them, sometimes on the phone, and would take down their names, location, and telephone numbers, too.

Dhan studied for two years, then came back to be with his family; later, he was released again to go to Korea for further study. This method of support continued for the second phase of studies until he came back and established his own ministry, which has also sought new unreached areas to work in.

In 2012, Dhan and Pratima decided to start a separate ministry. They have a mobile Bible school, church planting organization, and children's ministry, while Dhan lends a hand every week to Bible translation verification. Pratima still helps with media ministry follow-up and office paperwork with Philemon a couple of days a week. She is a very good teacher and helps with training pastors, and is following up her M.Div. with a Master's in Psychology (counselling). Dhan is completing his doctorate and working with Bible translators across the nation, making good use of his linguistic training in Korea. They are both very involved in ministry across the nation.

PHILEMON SPEAKS: HILL MINISTRY

Walking the hills is challenging. You may not get to a place to stay, especially on a longer multi-day hike, so you stay in caves, under trees, or find other shelter. It is enjoyable because the encouragement of people and pastors, with lots of preaching, makes this a different environment than city or plains work. Our vision has always been for the unreached in the hard places, so our churches are intentionally in the hills. The plains are easy places, but the hills are hard.

Dhan, Philemon and another team member did a lot of walking together. But as the work increased, Dhan and other friends continued this work while Philemon attended more to the work around Kathmandu.

PART SEVEN: HABIL'S MINISTRY

A NEPALI CHURCH SUPERVISOR UNDER PHILEMON

In 1991, Philemon met Habil.[19] Philemon had been asked by Prem to come from India to do some teaching in this new area of ministry.[20]

About 1991, there was a baptism service for thirty-nine people, performed by Philemon and Leonehart (a mission guest from the US). When the crowd saw this ceremony they took note of this group's change to following Christ. Also about this time, a woman named Charulata had a broken back caused by a nature god called Ahitabare. This god was angry at her because she was not able to meet its requests or demands.

People brought her to the church to pray for her. When they prayed to remove the demons from her, she saw a vision where a bat form within her left her body and then healing followed. Sixty-five families immediately decided to follow the Lord after they witnessed this. Habil was involved in ministry from this time onward.

---

19 Because their calendar is different, Philemon had to do some figuring to place the timing of this event. April 6, 2014 is the first day of 2072 according to the Nepali calendar.

20 Today, Habil's father has passed away, but his mother and brothers are still living in the same village.

PHILEMON INTRODUCES HABIL

If you had the opportunity to talk with Habil, Philemon says, you would want to set aside a good piece of free time. Habil has a lot of different testimony stories from years of ministry as an evangelist and church planter. When he goes to different places, sometimes blind eyes are opened, and sometimes lame people walk. That is his day-to-day life. Habil is the man God provided to supervise the ministry in south-central Nepal and oversee the work of the pastors and Bible study leaders. He has been a real asset, gifted by God for the work of the Gospel in this hill area.

HABIL'S STORY[21]

The work among the Chepang was started by a missionary from the Netherlands, who helped the Chepang when they didn't have any literacy skills. He had a real burden, so he hired a man who could help him translate the Bible into their language. This translator was Bhabikan. After translating and reading the verses for some time, and after many discussions as he worked together with the missionary, Bhabikan became a Christian. He and two other followers were persecuted—they were even tied up with ropes, beaten, and left half dead. But God was with them, and this was the beginning of his work among the Chepang people group.

---

21 The story of Habil demonstrates God's equipping of the church in leadership so that it continues to grow. Habil's own leadership has grown in many ways, and the editor was first able to meet this man on February 22, 2016. Philemon and a Canadian team, and Habil with his son Toshan on Habil's motorcycle, both drove to a central meeting spot and then spent a day of rest with Philemon's family. This included a two-hour personal interview with Habil during the late afternoon, with Philemon translating. Further contact has followed, at a two-day 2017 conference in the Chitwan area and a Kathmandu conference in 2018.

Some of the first Chepang believers came to brother Prem and asked for help in the ministry. Prem came to help, and in turn asked Philemon for further assistance even while he was still working in India. So Philemon helped with a seminar in this area. There were very few churches at this time in the hills of Chitwan.

An old man in Habil's area was an early believer, and shared the Gospel with Habil and others in his local area. The old man and his son have already died, but their work lives on. Habil was baptized in his early twenties by a non-Chepang brother who was one of the pioneer believers in this area.

Pastor Habil grew spiritually after his conversion, and feared the Lord greatly. As Habil attended meetings for new believers, he realized that he was missing out. The problem was that he couldn't read. The others read and studied different passages, and quickly learned much about their new faith. And they also sang songs from hymnbooks, while he had to memorize the songs. He had no way of learning more on his own.

Habil had never gone to school because his father had died early in his life. Now, he first needed to learn the alphabet, then some vocabulary, and so he prayed about this need: "Father, if You want me to study Your Word, then I will have to be able to read." And then the words began coming to him. Because he did not even have grade one as far as education goes, he also asked his friend to help him learn to read Nepali. His friends helped him to learn the alphabet and the names and books of the Bible. So over time, first in Nepali, then in Tamang, Habil learned to read and write. He now does some writing and reading in Chepang as well, and can speak Hindi orally. He sees answers to prayer as the most important factor in being able to read so he could grow in Christ and then minister to those around him. Sometimes he needs to write some reports, and while he is a little slow at writing, he has learned to carry out the tasks that are needed. He has even learned to use smartphones to record notes along the way.

Once Philemon started visiting his area, Habil became interested in working with him; shortly after, he was made area supervisor. He has worked alongside Philemon since 1996. The Lord confirmed his leading, as shortly after this time the Lord moved in the hearts of many Chepang, who became believers.[22] Habil's story illustrates the work of the supervisors in Philemon's ministry, though a few shorter profiles of other supervisors in other areas can be found in appendix three.

THE MAN WHO RUNS EVERYWHERE

Pastor Habil is a very dedicated man. Among all the Chepang Christians, he is one of the most faithful and trustworthy. Philemon told us some of the things that he greatly appreciates as a supervisor as seen in Habil's life. If you give him a time-sensitive responsibility, he finds a way to fit it into his very busy schedule. For example, just before Philemon's recent visit to Canada, Philemon gave Habil some money for uniforms for the school children. The uniforms were ready even before the students got back from their holiday time.

When one of his many house churches is ready to build a permanent meeting place, they confer with Habil to ask him how long it will take and what he advises. Then he will oversee the job

---

22 Habil became one of Philemon's busiest supervisors after Philemon took on Prem's ministry. Habil also ministers over a large area which takes him away from home about twenty days each month. An idea of what is involved starts sinking in when Philemon says that it can take three months to bring invitations to meetings and collect the answers, or get the earthquake damage information, to his then 105 (and now, just three years later, 117) churches. Ministry is not an easy task, and it requires a lot of travel by both foot and motorcycle. Habil is dedicated and courageous, and the Lord is using him mightily.

so that by the deadline, the local building team has finished the work and even produced a report with pictures.

Now, good reports are not something that you can expect in any country—even in Canada! But whenever Philemon asks for a special report about Habil's area, even if it takes several days, Habil takes the time to personally go there and collect details about what is going on. Habil sends the report to Kathmandu, or occasionally he comes himself—about eleven hours by motor-cycle—with the report from his area. He also maintains contact with Philemon by telephone when able. It took about a week and a half to find out how he was doing after the big earthquake in 2015, when his son was finally able to reach him by cell phone and get a report to Philemon.

Even while Philemon was in Canada, Habil phoned to tell Philemon about the death of an alumnus of the mission's Bible school who had ministered very well. Pastor Habil told Phile-mon, "There are almost two hundred members in that church in Makwanpur where the pastor died." They were so sorry to lose this faithful pastor.[23]

THE MAN WHO UNITES EVERYONE

Habil is very good at uniting the leaders who work alongside him from each of the churches and house cell groups in his area.

At times, other missions and agencies go to his area and tell Habil's leaders, "We will pay more money than you are getting now, so come work with us."

---

23 In 2002, the first pastor of that church, Pastor Praja, and eighteen members died from a mudslide; their bodies have never been found. Nineteen members of his family gathered for shelter in their pastor's home to be safe from the rain and flood, but on the evening of July 22, eighteen of them were buried in the mudslide in the pastor's home. One son was saved, and his name is Dabal.

Pastor Habil says, "If you want to go, you can go. But think about the future. Philemon's mission is continuing and has been here for over twenty years now." Because he has been such an important part of their life, they are willing to listen to his advice. Service to God and growing the Church as Christ's mission should be the motives of church planting, not financial ease.[24]

Many listen to Habil's advice. One time Philemon's mission was supposed to have their leadership conference in Siliguri, India. Philemon had arranged everything, and had asked Pastor Habil to bring some of the people there. Three hundred men and women, all of them church leaders, came down from the hills to the roadside at Habil's invitation, but there was a three day transportation strike which the Maoist party (communists influenced by the Chinese model) in the area had created. So they couldn't go until Philemon arranged buses from Siliguri to Habil's area. (Habil often manages to bring more people for less funds, so his teams can get as much training as possible.)

Habil has such a heart and such an ability that he can unite all the people of the area, not only the Christians. Giving advice and helping people makes him something of a social worker. If anyone needs a certificate or permit, Habil goes as soon as he can and gets it for them; so, everyone appreciates him, because he is very helpful. He is well-known in his area, and better off than others, because he has many fields to work.

---

24 This can be a problem overseas, where missionaries and pastors are often in subsistence financial situations. It is not uncommon for the missionary and pastoral staff of our partners to be approached by other ministries with an invitation to change their affiliation. Often the offer includes some kind of additional financial promise. Many ministries are growing because of financial abundance rather than genuine discipleship and effective ministry. Naturally, the unity between indigenous missions is damaged and ministry can become more of a competition than a matter of working together for the sake of the Gospel.

Here is an example that happened a couple of years ago. There are almost five hundred families from a village affected by a mudslide, living in a temporary camp that was also felt to be unsafe as rain continued. They moved from the temporary camp to the riverside, which was out of the path of the weakened hillside but in danger of being flooded due to the rains. The refugees had been ministered to during the whole process, and many had become believers.

A large portion of this displaced group, about 300–350, came to the Chepang school and moved into the cellar. Habil didn't know what to do with them, as they had already lost their homes and had only what they had saved in the rush of moving.

Pastor Habil had recently harvested some corn, and he fed these people with handfuls of it. If he had distributed the gift all at once, it would not have lasted long, so he gave it out little by little with water, and the corn let them survive. After some time, they went elsewhere.

Twenty-four families were helped by building temporary houses for them. The mission purchased the land with a little money, and built the houses near Habil's home. He also provided solar lights for them. A dozen families were rebellious so he gave them some money and told them to leave. The remaining thirteen decided that they would stay and were given proper deeds for the land, totaling one acre, as of January, 2016.

CELEBRATING AT A CONFERENCE

Through Habil's life of giving and ministry, many Maoists have come to know the Lord. In the past in a time of area-wide rebellion, he was captured and had to work hard for the Maoists. He had his Bible and steadily witnessed to them. God brought Habil into a place of influence through this, and later seven soldiers of the Maoist rebel group, who had been fighting against the government, put down their rifles and accepted the Lord because of his ministry.

One time the Maoists were ready to bury eight prisoners alive. They were digging the holes. Pastor Habil warned them to stop and they listened because he had some influence with their leaders in that area. The prisoners were so grateful that Pastor Habil had saved them through his courageous action. He continued going to the Maoist camps in different places and talking to the leaders while the uncertain times continued.

As others were transferred into his area, they have come to follow the Lord. Now the government has been able to come up with a constitution after about a decade of uncertainty. The country is still often ruled by minority coalitions, and India's Hindu influence is great, which are both factors in the governmental responses to Christianity in the country.

When Habil looks back over the last few years, he feels his people have been very blessed and it has been a time of much good change. As of 2018, he is supervising 117 churches, and he is also supervising the mission school for the Chepang, which keeps him very busy.

Habil confirms that he is home only about five to ten days in a month. The rest of the time he is out in the two districts he supervises. Habil also takes time to visit some churches in a new third district, where there are now three churches established. When possible, he tries to go to his own service on a Saturday, the men's service (Saturday is Nepal's Sunday). But other times he is out visiting different churches, encouraging them and teaching them. Philemon has frequently asked for prayer for this capable leader, who has so many responsibilities in this area of Nepal.

NEW CHURCH PLANTS

Habil regularly goes to new areas, accompanying groups of young people doing evangelism. They witness there, pray, preach, and come back. If anybody becomes interested, they will follow up. When people are ready for baptism, they baptize them there.

New churches are often started with this pattern: an unbelieving neighbour will ask a believer to pray to resolve some problem, such as for a miracle of healing. People are far too poor to go to a doctor, even if they are fortunate enough that there is one in their area. As soon as someone expresses belief in Christ, Habil goes there frequently to establish a Christian presence and community. He often grows the interest in a location by preaching in a one-room house. Several other families and singles come to hear the story, then start coming regularly. A more spacious place to meet is sought to enable further growth. After a period of time, if there are committed members, he prays and asks the most faithful person to lead the house-church group.

God also has his own ways and timing in adding churches. Habil and his leaders pray for the sick, and they often see healing take place. Habil related the following account about the latest church plant in 2016:

Lately, one man had a hand paralyzed to the elbow. When the local people from the nearest church prayed at his request, they did not receive an immediate answer, so they stopped praying. When I came, I heard about it and instructed the group that they should continue to pray. Then I prayed for the man and some movement came into his hand. I left shortly after, but as the church continued to pray, the arm and hand continued improving, and by the third day they were completely healthy.

As the two neighbouring families around heard and saw this, they joined the healed man in requesting to have teaching and are considering becoming Christians. I expect that soon a new church will form in that area.

As study groups mature, a new Christian leader is selected who will look after the work and the ministry. Pastor Habil trains the new leader slowly in whatever way he can. Most of the time, he sends several of his experienced people to do the training. It doesn't matter if they are educated or not—he will only appoint someone when they are ready. Sometimes, they can also attend the training school in Kathmandu for one month, or even for three months when that is possible.

Sometimes delegates come to the yearly area conference and recommend to Philemon that a certain man become an elder in the church. So Philemon will ordain him as an elder in his local area, and then the elder will look after the church.

Pastor Habil also plans to reach other outlying areas. It is due to this compulsion to reach out, and God's blessing, that he has over one hundred churches. It is his vision, wide outreach, and faithfulness over twenty-five years that have allowed him to add so many to the nineteen he began with.

NEW MOTORCYCLES: A REAL PASTORAL ASSET

Pastor Habil needed a new motorcycle in 2014. He had a second-hand motorcycle he had bought after saving up some money; it had been a very great help, but was getting old. He had been using it for three to four years, and it was worn out. When he came to see Philemon in Kathmandu, it took almost the whole day to travel with that old motorcycle.

Habil needed to buy a new motorcycle because it would help him to get to the trailheads, where he could leave it and continue on the walking trails. To climb such steep hills, a powerful vehicle is necessary. Pedal bicycles are indeed useful in the plains of India and Nepal. The pastors and missionaries there are very happy to get them, as they can travel more places and still get home for the night. But what is needed depends on the terrain, and in this case Habil needed a motorcycle to deal with the steep hills.

Philemon happily reported that an African person found out about this need and provided a new motorcycle in 2015. But it received so much use that it needed repair again about a year later. And in January 2018, Habil borrowed $3000 for a new and more powerful motorcycle when he came to visit Philemon. He had put so much use in hard terrain on his motorcycle that he needed a better one that would actually survive his work for more than a couple of years. However, funds did not come in to meet this need, and Habil is currently without a motorcycle. This is a need of many pastors working in the northern hill country of India and Nepal.

CHANGES IN THE CHITWAN AND MAKWINPUR AREAS TODAY

Travel has improved as roads are now being extended; more villages can be reached by Habil in fewer days as he carries out his work as church supervisor. When possible, he uses a motorbike from the trailhead that is a day's walk from his own home, although as noted, motorbikes wear out quickly on the hilly roads and are expensive to replace. Very recently, the Chepang from his village built a small house at the trailhead so there is a place for Habil and guests to sleep on their way in and out of the village. His wife does a lot of coordination and spiritual counselling ministry in their village while Habil is travelling.

In 2018, Dhan said that one pastor who used to take three complete days to walk to and from the early roads can now reach a bus point in a single day. Several pastors who came to a 2018 conference in Kathmandu had walked for two days, and a couple dozen more had walked for one day to reach a bus that drove nearly twenty-four hours to reach Philemon's church site. There are still many villages to which the shortest path is only wide enough for a single person, and the wider, more practical donkey trails are longer. This affects everything from bringing in cement and tin sheets for housing to the time it takes to evangelize. Roads reach nearer to these areas now, so that a motorcycle brings you near to the trails.

Cell phones are also bridging some of the gaps in communicating. Smartphones, motorcycles, and walking are equally important tools for the evangelists overseeing the work in this area. Technological solutions are not foolproof: you might still be more than a day's walk from your town to a road, and cellphones might lose their signal just by descending into the next valley. Today, much news does find its way to Habil's smart tablet, which he also uses as a Bible. This makes it easier for him to minister to the many churches he supervises. This is a big change for these forest hill people.

THE 2015 EARTHQUAKE

On April 25, 2015, there was a magnitude 7.9 earthquake near Kathmandu, the capital, in which nine thousand people were killed—the worst natural disaster in Nepal in eighty years. Philemon helped over three hundred families with the money he received from Canadian friends shortly after the quake.

The earthquake also directly affected the area Habil supervises. While that area is considered a secondary damage zone, up to 90% of the houses were damaged. Most were built of stones with mud inside and a concrete layer outside, because supplies are costly, in low supply, and it is very hard to bring them in. About eighty-five of the approximately one hundred churches in the area were damaged as well—some with major cracks, and others that completely collapsed. Some villages could still only be accessed by helicopter two months later, as the quakes and aftershocks damaged many trails with mudslides. The rainy season that started in May only compounded the problems. This was still true in the next year, as rebuilding continued at a very slow pace and the tents and tarps given in year one had started wearing out in the sun and wind.

When the earthquake happened, it took over a week for Philemon to find out where Habil was, and then only by contacting his oldest son, whose cell phone was in reach at the time. Habil had been out checking the damage and helping those in need, since many village homes in his area had collapsed.

When money for aid came from Canada, Habil immediately applied it to the ninety families most in need, choosing half who were not Christian. This was only the beginning of what still needs to be done, as there are many homes to rebuild, and about seven dozen churches as well, after this and the many aftershocks. By three years after the earthquake, only a handful of churches had been repaired.[25]

Pastor Habil is continuing to act as lead pastor in his home church. There are about three hundred believers there. He spends anywhere from five to ten days at home in a month, and

25 Due to new government codes, the church repairs now cost almost twice as much as previously. The benefit is that the churches become major community buildings, and they are therefore building them large enough for the expansion of the Church that will happen. Current costs are about $11000 for a building that will hold 100–150 (no chairs!).

is gone the rest of the time, covering areas within a two days' drive from his village, which used to be six days' walk. Habil's wife Magana acts as a mentor and counsellor in their home village, which is still a day's walk (nine hours) from the closest road. Magana is illiterate, but she actively advises women and children and encourages them from her hometown. The elders, pastors and congregants contribute to Habil's ministry as well.

Habil's son Toshan began sharing the ministry full-time by 2016. He takes care of whatever needs doing when Habil cannot be there. Toshan's wife Reena has had some Bible college training, and is helping in the work with the women. Reena lost a baby in early 2017, which also almost took her out with sepsis before they had an operation to take out the dead baby. Her recovery was difficult.

When asked about recent works of God, Toshan said that he had studied up to grade eight but was not fluent in reading even then. But since he has begun to help his father, by God's grace reading is actually becoming easy. And so this was to him the biggest miracle in answer to prayer that year.

Canadian friends were involved with a seminar in Jutpani in 2017, where we met Pastor Shyam, who is Toshan's father-in-law. We heard that in the last fourteen years this man has met all the neighbours on his road, and most have been led to Christ. Toshan spent part of the last year working in his area as an assistant after helping his father for some time. Jutpani is actually at the edge of the hills, in an area of fields and banana plantations.

Toshan is getting further training by working and assisting in his father-in-law's area, where there is a larger church. And so the leadership in Habil's ministry is being enlarged to answer the many calls for help in training new believers, preaching, and teaching.

Philemon now believes that there may actually be as many as several hundred churches in this area of Chitwan and

Makwanpur.[26] There is a new church started in Gorka state to join another two recently established there. There is also an elementary school in that area.

EPILOGUE

This story is not over. God is continuing to lead Philemon, his family, and his ministry teams in reaching out to the lost in Nepal and Northeast India. The Word is also going out through radio and television. The Holy Spirit continues to say "it is true" as people hear and read God's Word and teachings and receive answers to prayer. God has gathered these people together and grown them, and is calling new workers from among them to spread the Gospel news.

From a handful of believers in the 1960s to 850,800 in 2010 as noted in the book *Operation World*,[27] the Church in this region is still growing. God has promised His Kingdom would grow in every nation, and He is delivering on His promise.

---

26 Habil's story, as told by Philemon, was recorded in Canada in Bruce's living room on April 6, 2015. Further details and updates come from a personal interview in Sauraha, Chitwan, Nepal, Feb 22, 2016, and during times with Habil and Philemon in 2017 and 2018.

27 Jason Mandryk, *Operation World*, 7th ed. (Colorado Springs, CO: Biblica Publishing: 2010).

KIRIT'S STORY

The first time I met Kirit, I knew he was a man of the Word. It quickly became apparent from the stories he told and observing his interactions with others that this man's words, actions, and deliberations had been primarily influenced by time he had spent in God's Word. If you ever meet him, his charm and wit will immediately make an impression, but it is his humility which makes his ministry and witness particularly attractive.

Kirit grew up in a Hindu culture in northeast India. In his youth he considered Christianity to be a despised Western religion. Nothing but the work of Christ in his life can fully explain his radical transformation.

Jesus told the story of the Good Samaritan to illustrate the command to love one's neighbour. The neighbourly Samaritan would have likely been held in contempt by the recipient of his kindness in any other context. The shocking aspect of the tale was not the nature of the kindness shown, but the fact that the good neighbour was a Samaritan. Responding to Jesus' question, the pretentious Jewish lawyer only reluctantly approved of his actions (Luke 10). The impact of the story turned on the context.

And so it is with Kirit, who also crosses cultural boundaries in sharing the good news of Christ. Jesus' work in his life shines particularly brightly through the context of everyday ministry. Allow me to share a telling example. We were on our way to visit a rural church in Tripura, but needed to stop at a vehicle repair shop to drop something off before continuing on with the day's plan. Kirit stepped out of the car and began speaking with the repairman. As I watched from the front seat of the vehicle, their conversation suddenly burst into jovial laughter seasoned with a warm mutual kindness. What they shared in that brief moment would be typical of close friends passing time together over tea.

But these two would not typically be friends in Tripura. After my frequent travels to Bangladesh, it was not hard for me to discern this repairman as a Bengali. Among the indigenous tribals of Tripura, the Bengali are unwanted immigrants. With a population of 2.5 million,[28] the Bengali have risen to political and economic power, particularly since the Bangladesh independence war of 1971 when many Hindu Bengali flooded into Tripura. It is typical for the Borok—Kirit's people, numbering about 1.2 million in Tripura—to hold the Bengali in disdain.

When Kirit returned to the vehicle my expression must have communicated a question like, "What just happened out there?" Kirit knew that I was aware of the history of animosity between these ethnic groups. He turned to me with a look of great satisfaction and said, "They know that I love them."

How could this man come to love these invaders, his enemies? It is one thing to talk about loving one's enemies; it is another to exemplify it. Kirit would be the first to attest to the grace of God in his life as his motivation.

The Gospel has shaped Kirit's heart for the lost. He is an evangelist. Ever since he first met Christ and came to learn of his love and forgiveness, he has had a heart for his people—that they would come to know those same eternal truths which have become his life's foundation.

And there has been fruit. In 2015, Dr. Grant and I were invited to attend an annual convention of churches in the Khowai

---

28 Mandryk, *Operation World*.

district of Tripura. We met a number of the gathered church leaders, and Kirit introduced most of them as individuals with whom he had initially shared the Gospel. It was a joy to know that the 1,500 gathered at that convention were all no longer *"without hope and without God in the world"* (Ephesians 2:12, NIV) since Kirit's first travels there in 1977.

The story of Kirit's life and ministry in the following pages was relayed to me by him over the last four years. I have recorded this story to encourage you in how God continues to be at work in the world. I also hope that reading these pages will inspire you to partner, in one way or another, with Kirit in Tripura so that Jesus would become famous there.

—Brother Keith

PART ONE: BEGINNINGS

When Kirit was young, he was restless. He daily bowed down before the household idols and prayed, "Please give me real joy and peace!" But he was not finding it.

Kirit

Kirit was raised in the Indian state of Tripura in a rural village. Tripura is located in India's northeast, and its border is surrounded on three sides by Bangladesh. Kirit was the sixth child born to his mother and father, in a Borok family. The Borok are the dominant tribal group of Tripura, and they speak a language called Kok Borok.

Childhood in the village for Kirit was not unlike that of most other Borok children. He was often naughty. Whatever his family didn't want him to do, he did. Once Kirit was returning from his chores in the field and was hungry. He took a pineapple from the plantation and ate it to satisfy his craving. His eldest brother, who had charge of the plantation, learned that he had done this and beat him with a big stick. His brother was a very strict man and held the authority of his father in the home. In fact, Kirit was driven from their home for this act and was sent to stay with an uncle for a year.

While serving his year of punishment, Kirit spent much time in the fields following the cattle that his uncle owned. Curiosity got the better of Kirit—because he saw his uncle smoking, he decided to take up this habit himself, at the age of only seven. To Kirit, it seemed that everyone carried a pack of cigarettes in their pocket and engaged in this practice.

During his year with his uncle, Kirit was also introduced to drinking wine. Culturally, children were given money to go to the market to buy wine and other items. His uncle instructed Kirit to taste the drinks before purchasing them to make sure that he got the best quality bottles. This duty was frequent for Kirit, and caused him to become addicted.

At the end of the year when Kirit returned to his home, these habits continued. Homemade wine was readily available in the villages. Like most Borok women, his mother was also involved in making wine.

Life was utterly meaningless and hopeless for Kirit. He felt depressed and sought peace.

Kirit's father was a dedicated Hindu priest. He noticed that Kirit was searching, and since Kirit's elder brother was already married, he decided to make Kirit his disciple.

"After my death, you will be my successor. You will take care of these gods," his father told him. The Hindus in Tripura believe that unmarried people are holier for the family temple.

Daily, Kirit's father would take a bath, put on clean clothes and spend half an hour worshipping before the three household idols in their family temple. Kirit began to worship the idols when his father was absent, and he prepared himself to take over leading the worship in their home.

Kirit would bring a small, round, baked local sweet and a banana, and offer these items to the idols on a plate. He knew that the only way to satisfy the gods was to bring an offering. A person could not approach the gods empty-handed; if they did, their prayer would not be accepted.

The restlessness in his heart was evident in his repeated plea. "Give me real joy and peace in my heart," he would pray every time he approached the idols. "All I want is a life with hope and meaning."

Kirit remained unsettled in his soul. He attempted to satisfy his longing through drinking, smoking, and doing drugs, but he remained miserable. In outbursts of anger, he would retaliate violently against those who irked him.

He was also grieved by the injustices around him. He noticed that most of the rich people cheated the poor in order to make themselves wealthier. He thought to himself, "I must do something about this." He planned to join a gang in order to target the wealthy, take back what was not rightly theirs, and distribute it among the poor.

Kirit pursued a contact who he knew was involved in a very powerful gang. He was informed that before he could join the group, he would need to get six months' training. Before Kirit could pursue this path further, though, a book came into his life which would forever change him.

A NEW TESTAMENT

It was the time of Holi, the Hindu festival of colours. Kirit was in a playful mood like all the others, and went about the villages to neighbours and friends, chasing and colouring them with powders and coloured water.

Kirit, however, had a big surprise that day. He came to the home of one of his relatives in a nearby village in order to tease him with the playful ritual. He came to the door of his father's cousin, Shubbi, who was looking out the window, and prepared to get him with the colour.

Before Kirit could follow through, Shubbi was straightforward with him. "I do not play Holi. I am a Christian."

Surprised and fearful, Kirit ran away.

"Christianity is a Western religion," Kirit reflected to himself. Christians were a lower class than even the Muslims, and it would make Kirit unclean if he stayed near this relative.

Shubbi and his wife had become Christians ten years earlier when they went to Agartala, the capital city of Tripura. At that time, Shubbi was sick with asthma and his wife suffered from a tumour on her neck. They had pursued local medical treatment in the village, but nothing worked. Then they heard that a Christian doctor could possibly help and they decided to pursue it. At the Christian hospital in Agartala, they heard the Gospel and received Christ. They were some of the very first Christians among the Borok people.

In the days that followed his encounter with Shubbi, Kirit ran into him several times on the way to the market and also in the fields as they followed their cattle. Shubbi tried to take advantage of those opportunities to share the Gospel, but Kirit tried to avoid him. Shubbi thought Kirit might know how to read because he was in the eighth grade, so he decided to present him with a Bengali New Testament.

"What is this?" Kirit asked.

"This is the book—the Bible," Shubbi replied.

"What's a Bible?" Kirit probed further.

"It is the book about Jesus Christ," Shubbi said.

Kirit's love for reading and learning gave him an interest in reading the book. "Okay, I'll take it and read it," Kirit decided.

The next day, Kirit starting reading the Bible, even though he was busy with his school studies. Shubbi indicated to Kirit when he gave him the Bible that he couldn't understand it simply by reading it from beginning to end. Rather, he should give careful attention to the Gospels of John and Matthew. Other than that, Shubbi had not given any specific references for Kirit to examine.

The genealogy at the beginning of Matthew was not very interesting for Kirit, but he especially noted the last three verses in Matthew chapter 11. Kirit had read through Matthew, but the invitation of Jesus, *"Come to me, all you who are weary and burdened, and I will give you rest"* (Matthew 11:28, NIV), caught his attention.

Because his life had been so restless, this word about the rest offered by Jesus greatly comforted him. It seemed to be exactly what he had been searching for. As a result, just a few days after receiving the Bible, Kirit became extremely keen to read it. It had become thrilling to him.

The idea that Jesus would give Kirit his peace seemed clear enough to him, but he was troubled by two ideas that he found in

John 3:16. He would need to seek help in understanding what was meant by "everlasting life" and "perishing."

Kirit urgently sought out a meeting with Shubbi to ask him these questions. "Why will I perish? What does everlasting life mean?" After Shubbi tried to explain these things, Kirit took a few days to reflect on what he had heard.

BAPTISM

A few days after asking Shubbi his questions, Kirit heard that there would be a baptism taking place about two kilometres from his home village. A pastor from Agartala was coming to perform the baptism, because there were no churches in the region.

Kirit approached his mother secretly. "Mommy, I want to be a Christian," he said.

"No, no, no. Your father will be angry. Our society will not accept you, and you will suffer much. You are still young, only a child, and so you'd better not do this," she counselled him.

Kirit was restless. To him, time was of the essence. He wrestled with himself over the decision. His mother had discouraged him, and he knew he could not speak to anyone. But his heart was burning inside him.

On the morning of the baptismal service, Kirit went out early before breakfast to avoid a confrontation with his family. He walked to the next village and found twelve people preparing for water baptism in the pond. They were six couples ready to be baptized. Kirit took note that at sixteen years of age, he was much younger than all of them.

Horendro, an uncle of his father, was there and saw Kirit. "Why are you here?" he asked.

"I have accepted Jesus," Kirit said.

"Are you here to be baptized?" he asked.

"Yes," Kirit told him, surprising himself to hear that word coming from his mouth.

And thus Kirit joined the group.

The pastor was leading the service in this remote village, with approximately one hundred onlookers from the community. They came because they had heard that a Christian event was taking place. Kirit was baptized, and the new fellowship which was formed that day sang a few songs together. Shortly after singing, they were dismissed.

Kirit went home and told his mother that he had taken water baptism that morning. She remained silent about the matter, but was clearly not pleased that he had ignored the counsel she had given him a few days earlier.

Later that day, Kirit's father went to the market. There was a stir in the town because of the baptism. With so many people having witnessed the event, word had spread quickly to the neighbouring villages. At the market, his father learned that Kirit was one of the thirteen who had been baptized that morning.

Kirit's father came home that evening, confronted Kirit, and asked him, "I heard today that you were baptized. Is it true?"

"Yes," replied Kirit.

Frustrated with his son, he walked away and ignored Kirit until the next morning.

The next day his father called the family together, including several relatives, and they all sat down. They called for Kirit to come before them. The relatives were to serve as his father's eyewitnesses. He declared before them that Kirit was no longer his son and threw him out of the main house.

Kirit stayed in a small bamboo house that he had made for his studies. Typically, adults spent the evenings in the villages drinking local brew and getting unruly. Because education was such a serious matter, students would build these bamboo houses to provide some privacy so that they could focus on their studies. Kirit used the small study house as his temporary dwelling after he was kicked out of his father's home.

The next day, Kirit was beaten by his brother-in-law. Because word had spread that he was a Christian, he was beaten another time while he was out in the village.

Even while all these things were taking place, Kirit did not waver in his faith. He had started reading the Bible, and he took comfort in the promises of God written in it. At midnight he would go out into the pineapple and mango gardens in order to pray. It was very dark, but Kirit sought the Lord there in solitude.

During this time, Kirit made a point of walking around the temple with the family gods in it and praying to Jesus, "Lord, these are gods that wasted my energy and time, and never gave me peace." As Joshua walked around Jericho, Kirit walked around the temple and prayed that it would be demolished. A couple of weeks later, a storm with rain came and ruined the mud wall and sungrass-roofed structure. This event meant that his father could not worship there, so he made a small idol centre instead. His father did not learn the real cause of the temple's demise.

Two months later, Shubbi shared with the leadership of the Tripura Baptist Mission in Agartala that Kirit was suffering for the Gospel. The mission sent the baptizing pastor to Kirit's home to discuss the matter with his father. Because Shubbi was a relative, he did not come along; this would have caused a greater disturbance, and he would have been blamed for Kirit's decision to become a Christian.

The pastor approached Kirit's father and inquired about the young man.

"Shall we take Kirit?" he asked.

The answer was abrupt. "Yes, take him away. He is no longer my son."

Kirit then went to Agartala with the pastor to stay in a mission compound hostel for three years. While there, he studied in the local government high school.

PART TWO: HIGH SCHOOL, ITINERANT MISSIONARY, & RECONCILIATION

A YOUNG EVANGELIST

While Kirit stayed in Agartala, he took every opportunity to share about the Lord Jesus, especially with the other young students. There were many students in the city with whom Kirit made it his ambition to share the Gospel message.

Regularly on weekdays in the late afternoon, Kirit would visit the various high schools throughout the city. Kirit would seek permission from the principals of these schools to enter the campus. "I am here to visit several new friends, and would like to speak with them," Kirit would tell them.

The Lord's favour was on Kirit, and he was granted much freedom for his ministry. He always carried tracts with him, and distributed them broadly. Kirit would also use a little English to draw the attention of the students. Everyone was very interested in learning English, so they were fascinated by Kirit. They were curious to know how he learned the few words that he shared with them, because it was so rare to speak English in Tripura at the time.

On his visits to the various high schools, he would make follow-up plans with the students who were curious to know more about Jesus. He recorded their addresses and arranged to visit them in the boarding houses where they were staying. Then in the evenings and on weekends, Kirit would come and take time to share the Gospel. Students were eager to hear of this Jesus, about whom they had never heard before. A number of the students were beginning to respond.

ASSURANCE OF SALVATION

While Kirit was staying in the boy's hostel, he was keen to continue learning about what it meant to be a Christian. One day in mid-1972 he visited the Christian literature book shop on the mission grounds and came across a book that would cement his understanding of what Christ had done for him on the cross.

The title of the book, *The Marvels of Grace*, caught his attention while he browsed. This English volume was by Oswald J. Smith, then pastor of People's Church in Toronto, Canada, and Kirit decided to buy the book for a mere three rupees.[29]

Kirit dove right into the book and tried to complete it in the midst of a busy study schedule. He was impressed by the many Scripture passages that Smith quoted. It was a revelation to Kirit to learn that salvation is only found in the person of Jesus Christ. He was so relieved to learn that religiosity, attending church services, baptism, and every other activity had no bearing on salvation. This clarification helped Kirit understand that he could have assurance of salvation, and encouraged him greatly in the faith.

---

29 Equivalent to about 12 cents Canadian at the time.

A UNIQUE CLASSROOM OPPORTUNITY

Kirit had been praying for an opportunity to preach to his whole class in the government high school. He particularly wanted to present the Gospel to his teacher, who was a Bengali Hindu. So Kirit proceeded to make a plan, and the Lord blessed it.

He decided to take an English New Testament to school. Right before the afternoon leisure hour, Kirit planned to be the last one to exit the classroom. He had purposely written his name inside the New Testament so that it could be traced back to him.

After the leisure hour, the teacher arrived on time to teach his history class. All the students had gathered on time as per usual. Kirit had other plans, however. He surmised that if he came a few minutes late the teacher would have a couple minutes to look at the Bible and perhaps notice his name written in it.

Arriving to the classroom at the calculated moment of optimal potential, Kirit presented himself at the door. Typically, if students arrived late, they were required to request permission to enter the class.

"May I come in, sir?" Kirit politely asked of the teacher.

"Yes, yes, please come in," the teacher replied. Kirit proceeded to find his seat, but the teacher stopped him. "So, whose Bible is this?"

"Oh yes, this is my Bible," Kirit responded, seemingly unaware of how it had ended up on the teacher's desk.

"Are you a Christian?" the teacher inquired.

"Yes sir, I am a Christian," Kirit responded.

"Well then, today I will not teach my history class," the teacher said. "Kirit, you will be taking the class today and you will share about your Bible."

Kirit could see the Lord's favour on him. He had the uninterrupted attention of over twenty students and his teacher for the next forty minutes to share and preach Christ.

Afterward, several students approached Kirit, wondering how they could accept Christ and be baptized. Shortly afterwards, a large group of Kirit's contacts were prepared to declare Jesus Christ as their Lord and Saviour publicly.

Excited, Kirit went to speak with the evangelism director of the Agartala Mission Compound. He mentioned that some of his classmates and friends in the city wanted to be baptized. The director was thrilled at the news, and offered to provide transportation to and from the baptism location for the students.

Kirit and the evangelism director not only spoke about transportation, but also discussed a strategy about where to carry out the service. The baptism could have taken place in Kirit's mission compound, but then it would have been inside a closed facility without any witness to the surrounding community. They mulled over finding the most public place in Agartala so that the news of this event would spread rapidly throughout the city.

The two concluded that the best place was at the Assam Rifles Ground, a military base where there was a small hut constructed by a few of the Christians in the regiment for their regular worship. Some of the servicemen stationed there were from other parts of India and were Christians. Next to the makeshift church building was a pond.

The director gave money to Kirit to arrange travel for the baptismal candidates. He also provided some funds to arrange transportation for witnesses to attend. Some of those with whom Kirit had shared the Gospel were not yet ready to accept Christ, but they were interested in witnessing the event. There were about fifty non-Christian witnesses who attended the baptism that day.

The forty-four students who were baptized joined the fellowship that gathered on the Assam Rifles Ground, remaining a part of that congregation until they graduated from their respective schools and returned to their home villages throughout Tripura.

THE HERALD TEAM IS FORMED

Kirit's passion for sharing the Gospel continued to be heavy on his heart. Having these forty-four young people come to Christ was a huge joy, but it was only the beginning of an answer to his prayer. He was praying that the Lord would not take him home until he saw fifty percent of his people, the Borok, professing faith in Jesus Christ. He knew, however, that he could not do the work on his own.

Kirit found several other youth who stayed in the hostel on the mission compound. He said to them, "Here we are inside this mission compound while there are thousands of people just outside of these walls with no one preaching to them. Let us do something." Kirit was realizing that God was calling him and his friends to take the message of salvation to the Borok people.

He began an evangelistic team with three other students in order to proclaim Christ throughout the city of Agartala. The three who enlisted were some of the earliest believers from other ethnic tribes, just as he was one of the very first among the Borok people who came to faith in Christ.

Every Saturday and Sunday evening for three years, the Herald Team, as they called it, would go out singing songs, distributing tracts and sharing the Gospel with different groups of people throughout the city.

ITINERANT EVANGELIST

Kirit baptizing believers. His ministry of evangelism through friendly
conversation results in many such occasions

In April 1975, Kirit departed from the hostel after his final examination. Unlike the other students who returned to their villages
after graduating high school, Kirit had no home to go to. This was
not a particularly heavy burden for Kirit, because he was learning
to trust his Heavenly Father, who faithfully took care of him.

Kirit's passion remained in evangelism. What Kirit had not
realized earlier was that the Lord was orchestrating His plan to
open the door for Gospel proclamation throughout the state. The
youth who had accepted Christ and been baptized at the Assam
Rifles Ground in 1973 had now returned to their homes in different parts of the state, and were sharing their faith in their villages.

Kirit began receiving invitations to come and preach the
Gospel wherever these students were. It became evident that

this itinerant ministry was part of God's plan. Kirit would spend much time between 1975 and 1977 travelling from Agartala to various places throughout Tripura, preaching the Gospel and seeing the Lord bring in a harvest of souls.

While Kirit was in Agartala, Ramesh did all that he could to help Kirit in his ministry. This continued in some measure until Kirit's time at Bible college. Ramesh was a brother in Christ from the Borok people group who served as an evangelist with a large Baptist group. He was stationed at their compound in Agartala. Ramesh would provide lodging, a little food, some used clothes and sometimes a few rupees to assist Kirit in his itinerant ministry.

WITNESSING IN SOUTH TRIPURA

One week after finishing high school, Kirit received a call from Cahran, one of his classmates who had returned to his home in a district in the far south of Tripura. Cahran had become a Christian in Agartala through Kirit's witness and sharing in high school. He asked Kirit to come in order to share the Gospel. Kirit decided to take his good friend Raj along with him, even though he did not speak Kok Borok, because he was a faithful companion in his evangelistic ministry.

One major obstacle the two young men faced was that they had no money to travel. So, Kirit and Raj began to pray. "Lord, we only have ten paisa. We need 240 times as much to travel down to Charan's place in order preach the Gospel there." Kirit and Raj prayed for several hours and then went to bed.

In the morning, Raj said to Kirit, "I have an idea. Wait here. I will be back shortly."

Raj went to tell a Christian family that he knew that Kirit and he had a plan to visit the far south of Tripura in order to preach the Gospel. He explained to them that as of the night before he and Kirit had only ten paisa in hand and they needed twenty-four rupees in order to travel there.

The family was happy with their plan and gave them ten rupees toward their travel expenditure need. They now had one hundred times their original amount.

By faith, Kirit and Raj began to pack up. With bags in hand, before they departed from the mission compound, the wife of the mission's general secretary noticed the two young men preparing to travel somewhere. She was working in her kitchen, which faced the exit gate of the compound, and she called out, "Raj! Come here."

Raj put his bag down and went to the kitchen door.

"Where are you going?" she asked.

"We are going to a village to preach the Gospel," he answered.

"Wait one minute," she told him. "I have some rupees for you. When my husband goes to the market he brings me the spare paisa, and I have been putting them aside in a box here. You can take them. It may be helpful for you. I think I've collected about fourteen rupees now."

Raj simply smiled and thanked God silently for His amazingly precise provision.

Sure enough, inside the change case the needed fourteen rupees were sovereignly prepared.

Raj thanked the pastor's wife and returned to Kirit with the gift in hand and a big grin on his face.

"Here Kirit, we now have twenty-four rupees. It looks like we have ten spare paisa for our travel."

The two young men left the mission compound praising God, and went on their way with His provision in hand.

Kirit and Raj travelled south and came to the village of their high school classmate. They connected with Cahran and began a three day campaign to share the Gospel. They would visit and share with people during the day, and call together a meeting in the evenings.

A crowd gathered in that village and Kirit preached the Gospel. On the second night Kirit made an altar call, and eleven young people came forward to accept Christ.

Because Kirit was not yet an ordained minister, he asked Cahran if there was any pastor or missionary in the area. Cahran mentioned that there was a missionary from Mizoram who had just started working about eleven kilometres away, and that they could call for him. Early the next morning, they sent for the missionary, who came to baptize this new group of believers.

These eleven new believers formed a new fellowship, and it became the first church to be established in that village in South Tripura. Through this church, many new congregations were established as the Gospel spread from there.[30]

BEGINNING TO CONNECT WITH FAMILY

While Kirit was travelling throughout Tripura, when close to home he would take the opportunity to visit his mother, continually sharing Christ with her. In 1976, Kirit's mother and youngest brother accepted Christ. His mother, however, suffered for the Gospel and was beaten a number of times by Kirit's father for her decision.

In 1977, when Kirit popped in to see his mother, his father approached him and said, "I want to speak with you. Come and see me later."

---

30 As of 2017, there are about thirty churches in the area.

Kirit went to go present himself to his father to hear what he had to say.

"Your mother and your brother have now accepted your Christ. Why are you doing all these things?" Kirit's father demanded. "It will be better for us all if you leave your Christ and come back home."

Kirit respectfully responded to his father, "Please, let me share a little about my Jesus with you."

He then proceeded to lay out a number of points in order to reason with his father. "For nine years I worshipped our family gods, and they never once returned anything to me. I tried to get peace and joy, but I was always empty. You told me that this is a god and that is a god. But they are not moving. They are just sitting in one place, not talking or hearing. You must know that Jesus has now given me His peace. Jesus has given me complete forgiveness and eternal life. After death, where will you go? Now I know my place; where is yours? Who gives you a guarantee? I have a guarantee. My Jesus is already in heaven and He is coming back. He is there now preparing a place for me, a heavenly home."

His father could not respond and simply remained silent. He listened to everything that Kirit had to say.

Kirit continued to share. "You see this Bible—this is the Word of God. It tells us everything that He has in His mind, all He has spoken for you and for me. Everything from A to Z."

His father continued hear Kirit out. After a short pause he said, "I do believe in your Jesus Christ." While the confession was not a serious commitment, this conversation was the beginning of some communication between Kirit and his father.

PART THREE:
MARRIAGE AND MINISTRY IN KHOWAI

APPOINTED TO THE MINISTRY

A leader with the large Baptist group in Agartala approached Kirit one day and asked him what he thought about being appointed to ministry with them.

"Actually, I am already called by the Lord to the ministry," Kirit replied. "I am happy to do this work whether or not you give me an appointment. To be appointed as an evangelist with this group is only a bonus for me; it would be a blessing. I will not do the work because they have appointed me, but I would be doing it regardless."

Kirit was first appointed by the association for a two month period in 1977. He continued to spread the Gospel, and they called him once more. This time they wanted to send him to another district.

MINISTRY IN A NEW PLACE

Eager to share his faith with the many Tripuri who had never before heard the Gospel, Kirit was commissioned to serve as a missionary in the new district.

In this new area, rural travels were quite dangerous because an outsider could be killed at any time. For this reason, Kirit began his ministry in the district capital where it was a little safer. But even there, no one accepted him because he was from another district. There were two government high schools in the community with boarding houses for students who came from all over the state for their studies. Kirit was able to stay in one, even though he was not a student. In this way he gained safety and acceptance. Although the students were fine with him being there, someone warned him that because he was not a student, he would not be able to stay there for long.

Kirit spent most of his time travelling throughout the district, despite the risks of doing so. One village was identified to him before he went to the district because there was a family there who had become Christians years earlier. When he arrived in their town, he found that the family had backslidden and was no longer living to serve the Lord. Kirit spent some time in the village, preaching and calling people to repentance. They began to respond, and in November 1977, twelve people were baptized. God continued to use his servant Kirit to work in the people's hearts.

A few months later, one of the friends that Kirit had made in the previous city invited him to attend a wedding in a nearby village. It was a very strict communist area. Kirit was excited to attend a wedding and have an opportunity to share with new people in a new area.

Wherever there were people gathered together, Kirit would go and sing gospel songs and share with them. Not surprisingly, in the village where the wedding was there were those who took offense to him. A group of communists made plans to kill Kirit on the night of the wedding. If anyone were to say anything against the communists, they would typically meet an untimely end.

The bride's uncle came to Kirit trembling during the evening. He took Kirit outside the house to inform him of what was going on.

"Brother, you must leave immediately," he urged Kirit.

"What is going on?" Kirit wondered.

"They are already preparing your burial ground. They are ready to kill you."

Before Kirit could even partake of the wedding meal, this uncle hastily escorted him through the dark jungle to a village about six kilometres away. God had His hand on Kirit, and watched over him during this dangerous time in ministry in the district.

Kirit stayed one night in the nearby village, and departed the next morning.

IN NEED OF A HELPMATE

Before Kirit had gone to the new district as a missionary, he had decided that he would remain celibate in order to fully give his life for the Lord's work. He was a passionate young man in the service of his King.

Not long after Kirit was sent there, he became so sick with headaches and high fever that he could not eat or even drink water. One of his distant relatives, who also lived in his boarding house, tried to help him by cooking and by applying green chilies to his head where he had some swelling.

When he recovered from his sickness, Kirit realized the benefits of having a helpmate in the ministry. He prayed and said, "Lord, this experience was a revelation to me. I understand now that I need a suitable helper."

Finding a suitable wife was no small thing. Kirit had previously tried to find a wife on his own, but three times he had been rejected. He hated to face the possibility of a fourth rejection. If he married, he would need a wife who was a Christian, who would join him and come alongside him in missionary work. He would need a wife who was content to be poor. It would not be easy to find someone, but God had a plan.

A few months later, Kirit went to preach the Gospel in a new village.

"Are you married?" asked an elderly man, whom Kirit had come to know as "Grandpa."

Puzzled slightly by this man's straightforward question, Kirit replied, "No."

"Do you want to get married?" Grandpa asked.

Not sure where the conversation was going, Kirit joked with him, "If I find someone suitable, I will get married."

"Well then," began Grandpa, "there is one young lady here and another one there." Grandpa suggested a few girls to Kirit, one of them being a young woman named Tarumala. "Can you visit one of them?"

Among the Borok people, *visiting a girl* is somewhat similar to proposing.

"I am unprepared," Kirit said. "I should not go." He had only seven rupees in his shirt pocket, and some kind of a gift is expected along with a *visit*.

Grandpa responded to Kirit, "Instead of an arranged visit, why don't you go with my son then?" Grandpa's idea was that Kirit could stop by the girl's house as if he was simply spending time with a friend and use that opportunity to see if he might like to pursue things further.

Kirit would soon learn that Grandpa enjoyed meddling in the affairs of others, particularly trying to arrange relationships.

Kirit happily went with Grandpa's son to visit Tarumala's family's home. Shortly after Kirit's arrival there, Tarumala went to the market to purchase a few things for the family dinner, which was her normal duty, so the two of them barely even saw each other.

Later that evening, the family was surprised to learn that Grandpa had been telling the rest of the villagers that a young man had come to see Tarumala. Culturally, everyone knew this was the first step for a young couple to consider marriage. Tarumala was shocked and asked, "Why wasn't I informed? How did he come?"

Grandpa responded and said, "I informed him but he was not ready. So he just came to see your house. While he was here, he saw you."

Before leaving the following day, Kirit was met by Grandpa, who informed him with a smile, "You know that girl... she is quite happy. She heard that you came and saw her."

"How did the news come out?" Kirit asked in surprise.

"I told her. You should not worry," the elderly man encouraged Kirit.

"Okay then. Let me pray to see if God is willing. One thing that should be known is that I am a Christian. She too must be a Christian—otherwise I will not marry her."

Grandpa went to inform Tarumala's parents. They, however, could not agree to such a marriage. They were *paka* (very orthodox) Hindus.

"This is impossible," Tarumala's father protested. "She is my eldest daughter and I am the political leader here. People will talk negatively if I give my daughter to a Christian in marriage."

Grandpa now had become the mediator in the back and forth between Kirit and Tarumala's family. He came to Kirit and said, "This is a very difficult requirement that you have. They will not accept it."

Kirit replied, "I cannot reject Jesus. I will reject Tarumala if I must, but I will never reject Christ. You go and talk to them again."

The elderly man returned to speak with Tarumala's parents. The parents then called for Tarumala and asked her, "Have you seen the boy?"

"Yes. I saw him for a few minutes. He came with his friend but I did not know that he came in order to see me."

The parents decided to call for Kirit and speak with him in person. It turned into a long discussion.

Finally, Tarumala's father proposed to Kirit, "I am a political leader in this town. Can you please become a Hindu so we can perform the Hindu marriage here? After getting married, you can both become Christians."

Kirit, trying very hard to respect them, thanked Tarumala's father for the proposal. However, he replied, "I want you to know that I too am a very honoured person with great status. But my status is not before men, like yours. My Creator God, my Saviour Jesus Christ—He honours me, loves me and respects me."

Tarumala's parents were completely silent and did not know what to say.

After a seemingly awkward silence, Tarumala's father said, "Okay then. Let us just go our own way from here."

Kirit responded, "Wonderful. This is fine with me. For your daughter, there are many boys out there. For me, if my God has a plan for me to get married, He will bring it to pass."

One month later, Grandpa was back to his old tricks and came to Kirit with another proposal.

"Why don't you hold your marriage ceremony in Agartala, and then come back to our village for a reception celebration?" the man proposed.

"I am not a thief," Kirit clarified, "that I should do everything secretly so people do not see what I am doing. I am willing to get married here openly. Otherwise I would rather not get married at all."

"Alright then, but why don't you come again and we can discuss the matter once more with Tarumala's parents?" the man persisted.

Again Kirit met with Tarumala's parents. The father proposed to him, "Go have the marriage in Agartala in your Christian church and we will pay for the wedding there."

Kirit declined the generous proposal, even though he had no money and it would have been a big help for him. "If God wills, everything will be open and we will have the marriage here. I cannot do it in a hidden way."

The marriage negotiations once again came to a halt.

In April, Grandpa again came to Kirit.

"I feel very embarrassed," the elderly man confessed to Kirit. "Could you please reconsider the proposal arrangement one more time?"

"Sorry, I cannot consider it again. Tarumala must receive Christ and be baptized; otherwise, I will not marry her." Kirit was firm in his position, but he desired to connect with her personally. "I have a request for you," Kirit told the elderly man. "Could you please arrange for me to meet with Tarumala one-on-one for about thirty minutes?"

Grandpa was excited to see the potential for progress in this matter, and arranged for them to meet in a sweet shop in the market.

Tarumala came with her friend to meet with Kirit.

"Why have you called me?" Tarumala asked.

"I want to share my heart with you. If you agree, I am ready to get married. Otherwise not." Kirit then shared the Gospel with her. Curious about one thing after his presentation, Kirit asked, "Do you love me?"

"Yes," Tarumala responded.

"Why?" Kirit almost interrupted her brief response. "I am a Christian."

"Actually, I have been searching for a man who is free from drunkenness, from smoking and drugs. So you are the right man. I like your behaviour, conduct, and life," she said.

"Do you only love me for this?" Kirit wondered.

"No. I have also studied your Bible and your tracts. One of my classmates in college is a Christian, and she has shared these things with me. I want to accept your God, but my parents do not agree. Teach me how I can pray."

"Simply pray, 'Jesus, I receive you. Come into my heart,'" Kirit instructed her. "Humbly ask God, saying, 'I want to get married; please open the door and provide the opportunity.'"

"Do you demand anything?" Tarumala nervously asked. Customarily, the groom requested a dowry, which was often a burdensome amount for the bride's family.

"I demand nothing. No money, no land, no nothing. I simply desire to be married to you," Kirit replied.

Tarumala was delighted to hear this. Her family was struggling financially, particularly because her father had spent much money pursuing politics and running in last year's state election, and they didn't have anything.

Tarumala went back to her parents and mentioned to them that Kirit did not demand any dowry. Her parents were conflicted—Kirit's position was very counter-cultural. They were nonetheless very happy.

Tarumala's parents then called for Kirit. Grandpa was not there this time. He had gotten very discouraged, and had given up on the situation. So a new mediator took his place.

When they got together again, Tarumala's father needed to ask Kirit the question himself. "Kirit, do you demand anything?"

"No, I don't have any demands," Kirit replied.

"Where do you plan to live after you get married?" Tarumala's father asked.

"If you agree, she and I will live here, together with you," Kirit suggested. He didn't have a house himself, and he couldn't take Tarumala back to his father's home because he had been expelled from his family.

The plan seemed satisfactory to Tarumala's parents and they said, "Okay, let us now make plans for the wedding."

Tarumala's parents were not excited about their daughter marrying a Christian or holding a Christian marriage in their home. They were very committed Hindus, but out of love for their daughter and their desire for her to be happy, they consented to the event and gave it their okay. They were, however, planning to try to reconvert Kirit and Tarumala after the wedding was over.

There was a rumour circulating that was interfering with the marriage plans. Kirit's home village was 150 km away, and some people were saying that he already had a wife and three children back home. To ensure that their marriage was honourable and a good testimony, Kirit knew that he needed to have witnesses to confirm his singleness.

He ended up communicating with his parents, and urged them to attend the wedding. Because of the broken relationship, they were not willing to contribute anything to the marriage ceremonies. They did, however, attend the wedding in the new district at Tarumala's family's home to attest that their son could lawfully wed. This was facilitated by an offer by Tarumala's parents to provide a vehicle to pick them up and bring them back to their home.

Prior to the wedding, Tarumala was baptized publicly in the pond by her home, as a confession of her faith in Christ and commitment to living her life in His service.

The wedding day finally arrived. Kirit and Tarumala were married on May 9, 1978.

Kirit and Tarumala

FIRST FRUITS OF MINISTRY

Even while living in the home of Tarumala's family, Kirit continued to travel and share the Gospel in different parts of the district. Shortly after their marriage, the Lord demonstrated His grace mightily and provided the first fruits of ministry in this area. Forty-five young people from the schools where Kirit was preaching accepted Christ and were baptized in the town pond.

News of Kirit's activities spread, leading to unease in the town. A local newspaper published stories accusing Kirit of being a foreign influence working for the CIA and the Mizo terrorist group that was active in Tripura. They alleged that he was there to steal the hearts of the young people and turn them away.

This caused a disturbance in the town. Twice people tried to coordinate ambushes against Kirit to kill him. However, the Lord continued to protect him.

RURAL MINISTRY

The Lord was at work and opening doors before Kirit. As a result of the mass conversion of the forty-five students, many rural villages opened up throughout the state. These students returned to their homes and shared with the villagers that they had become Christians. Word spread quickly in many places.

Kirit travelled to the interior to share the good news of Christ. At one particular village, he found shelter with a man of peace. Walking through the village, he found forty people gathered together in an open rice paddy field. At first they thought he was the young prince, Kirit Bikram, who was running for a seat in the Parliament of India with the prominent Congress Party.

"I am not a Congress man," Kirit corrected them. "I have just come to tell you about Jesus Christ."

The local communist leader reacted immediately. "You must leave our village in the next hour; otherwise, there will be trouble for you!"

Kirit knew this was no small threat—they might even kill him if he didn't take heed. But God gave him encouragement in his spirit.

"You are here, Lord," he prayed silently. "Take control of the situation."

Surrounded by the group of forty, Kirit requested just five minutes to speak. They said no.

"Just give me four minutes then," he quickly suggested. "After I'm done, you can kill and bury me if you want."

So Kirit proceeded to share the Gospel. After twenty minutes had passed, no one had said anything, so he continued on for another five minutes.

"Okay, okay," they responded once he had finished. "Now we understand. We will meet with you again sometime."

The crowd dispersed and went on their way.

Kirit left that place and came to another village about five kilometres away, where ten people sat drinking local wine together (which is very common in the villages).

He approached the group. "May I join you?" Kirit asked.

"Who are you?" one man asked with a low, arrogant voice.

"I am Kirit."

"What do you want here?"

"I'm here to share my faith with you."

"What faith is that?" the man demanded.

"Jesus Christ."

"We don't want to hear of it. We will shed your blood."

An elderly man heard what was going on and came out. "Why are you shouting?" he asked.

"This man here, he came to preach his Jesus," said the arrogant leader.

The old man nodded. "He can preach. What is the problem with that?"

"No," insisted the leader. "If he shares his faith with us, we will kill him."

"I want to say one thing," Kirit said. "If you shed my blood, I will be happy. I'm ready to have my blood shed for Christ and for my own people. But before you kill me, can you please allow me to share for a few minutes privately?"

They group agreed and decided to meet in a nearby house.

He sat in the middle of the group and talked for a while, asking them what they received from their Hindu religion. Then Kirit shared about the previous emptiness in his life and how he had once been a drunkard himself.

"Now I don't care about any of these things," he said, "because Jesus has given me His peace for all my spiritual and mental problems."

"Yes, this is the right way!" someone shouted.

Another turned to this man and asked, "Oh, so you want to become his follower?"

They began to fight with one another. One group supported Kirit and another opposed him.

"Don't fight," Kirit said to them. "Please, don't fight. Fight for good things. Don't fight amongst yourselves." He then left that place.

Six months later, a church was established in that village.

AN ATTEMPT TO CHANGE THEIR MINDS

Approximately nine months after their wedding, Kirit and Tarumala learned of a spell that her parents were trying to cast upon them. Tarumala's sister informed the young couple that their parents had sacrificed a goat at one of the temples, and that the gods were going to come to make them forsake Christianity for Hinduism.

The parents even sent some Hindu priests to Kirit and Tarumala to try to change their minds and break up their marriage. However, when Kirit realized what was happening he declared to the priests, "No, this is not possible. You must leave."

Tarumala's parents eventually gave up their attempts to try to convert Kirit and Tarumala, and made them move out of their house instead. This was an attempt to save face in the community. But Kirit and Tarumala remained in her village, and constructed a simple bamboo house to live in.

VISIT TO HIS HOME

Sometime later, Kirit travelled to his home village to see his parents, since his father had suggested that he bring his wife and their baby daughter for a short visit. Because the relationship with his parents had begun to warm, Kirit thought it would be good for them to get to know his growing family. They agreed, and Kirit brought Tarumala and the baby for a ten-day visit. Kirit's father was especially impressed with Tarumala's cooking and enjoyed their time together. An arrangement was made for the family to return during the summer vacation in June.

PART FOUR:
TIMES OF TESTING AND GROWTH

Tarumala received an opportunity to enroll in teacher training in Agartala. While she studied there, the mission with which Kirit was serving full-time learned of the situation and thought that the family should be together. They invited Kirit to Agartala to take part in a missionary training course.

When it came time for summer vacation, Kirit went to his wife's village to get his daughter, who had been staying with

Tarumala's parents. He travelled directly from there to his home town. On her own, Tarumala travelled to join them from Agartala. Kirit himself did not have any vacation time, so he was going to just bring his family to his parent's village and then return immediately to Agartala to continue with his missionary training. After dropping off his family, Kirit went to the market in a nearby town, in order to catch transportation back to Agartala.

KIRIT'S LIFE IS SPARED

Kirit was feeling a little uneasy about going back to Agartala. Before leaving, he decided to visit his nephew, Gedu, who lived nearby.

"Gedu, I'm feeling unsettled about going to Agartala and I'm not sure why," Kirit said.

"Well, okay then. Just keep your bag at my place and let's go have some tea," Gedu responded. "Whenever you are ready, you can easily come back here to get your bag and go on your way. It's not far."

Kirit put his bag down and they went to the market to have tea together, as is the custom in Tripura.

While they were catching up over tea, vehicles from the southern part of the province, filled with Bengali women who were crying and wailing, began entering the town. Everyone came over to ask what was going on, and a great commotion ensued.

"We are being attacked by the tribals!" the Bengali women cried. "They are burning our houses and killing us."

The many Bengalis in the market town became incensed when they heard this news.

In the midst of all the commotion, Kirit and Gedu quickly left the market. Kirit collected his bag and rushed back to his village to inform his family of what was happening.

From June 6 to 8, 1980, communal violence erupted in Tripura between Bengalis and tribal peoples. Kirit and Tarumala, along with many others throughout the northeast Indian state, hid in the jungle in order to avoid the terror and bloodshed. Tension and fear characterized society in the months that followed the violence.

Reflecting on all the events, Kirit looked back on his hesitation to go to Agartala. He was sure that if he had embarked on his journey, he would have been one of those who were killed. He knew that the Lord, however, had spared his life.

Near the end of June that year, while there was still an air of apprehension throughout the state, a relative of Kirit conspired to kill him. Each night as the violence continued, different family members took turns on the night watch. In his birth town, there was a Bengali family who lived nearby, and Kirit's family didn't feel safe.

This relative was particularly infuriated with Kirit because of his Gospel work. He thought that if he killed Kirit then Christianity would be abolished in their area. He tried to secretly organize a group to carry out the attack by approaching different individuals one by one and convincing them that this needed to be done. They intended to carry their plan out while Kirit was on one of his night watches.

One cousin happened to learn of what was going on. He told the relative not to touch Kirit, or a bigger problem would come upon him. It was not long after this warning that the scheming relative contracted a disease and died. The cousin informed Kirit about all these things after the relative's death.

CORRESPONDENCE WITH BILLY GRAHAM

Kirit had a friend in the ministry who was receiving a subscription to *Decision*. Before seeing a copy of the magazine for himself, Kirit had never heard of Billy Graham. His friend mentioned that if he wrote in and requested a copy of the magazine, he too could receive it. The advice proved true.

Kirit came to learn how effective the Billy Graham Association was in its work. His friend gave Kirit another booklet about the association's ministry around the world. He learned that they even had two associate evangelists in India. Interested to learn more, he found out that these men were honourable and godly servants of Jesus Christ.

Kirit wanted to become more effective in ministry like these men. He decided to write a letter in 1981 to Billy Graham with one question: "How can I be a very effective and simple evangelist?" A letter came back from the evangelist's pen with three recommendations for Kirit to implement. Reverend Graham suggested that Kirit discipline himself to wake up early in the morning, read the Bible, meditate and pray.

The first thing that Kirit did was to get himself an alarm clock. He set his alarm for 3:00 a.m. In fact, Kirit did this for the next sixteen years. He would take three hours each morning to be with the Lord and seek Him in His Word.

Kirit decided to follow up with Billy Graham and ask him a second question. He wrote to ask if he could become an associate evangelist with the Association in India. Reverend Graham responded again, and told him that he did not have the theological qualifications necessary to be an associate evangelist.

Kirit could understand the response he received. He, however, did not really want to pursue theological training. He simply moved on and did not further pursue service with the Association.

JESUS HEALS KIRIT

In 1983, Kirit began to have serious health problems. He was admitted to the Agartala hospital for thirteen days because his body was swelling and in great pain. To make matters worse, while Kirit was suffering in the Agartala hospital he received the news that his father had passed away. He was not able to attend the funeral, and he was very troubled over his father's death. He was very worried about his eternal state.

The doctor diagnosed Kirit with a kidney problem and indicated that he would likely need surgery. The hospital there did not have the facilities or professional expertise to perform the surgery, so Kirit would need to consider other options. He remembered that one of his brothers had suffered from a similar condition and died when he was younger.

Kirit and Tarumala decided to seek out medical help in South India at the famous Christian hospital in Vellore, founded by missionary Ida Scudder. The two travelled there on a twenty-six day journey.

Upon their arrival in Vellore, the doctor ran a number of tests on Kirit. He came back and told Kirit that they had tested his kidneys, blood, and liver, and could not find anything wrong. "Praise the Lord," the doctor said, "we didn't find anything."

Kirit replied, "No, you must do more tests. I'm still suffering."

"We don't need to check again and again," replied the doctor. "We have tested everything, and haven't found anything."

Kirit showed them his swelling, which was still evident, but the doctor said that nothing could be done.

The pain kept increasing and intensifying. At the Kolkata airport on the journey home, the pain became unbearable. Kirit told Tarumala. "You'd better go home, and I'll return to Vellore on my own."

Tarumala replied, "Let's go back to Tripura. God is just as present there as He is in Vellore."

Kirit complied with her suggestion and they flew back to Agartala, returning near the end of March, 1983.

Nothing improved, even though Kirit tried everything he could, including some herbal medicine. The pain eventually disappeared, but the swelling continued and became extreme. Kirit grew weaker and weaker.

He finally gave up hope. Several weeks after his return from Vellore, he told Tarumala that she should not be surprised to find him dead the next morning.

After a few minutes of difficult silence she shared, "Let me say something. You are praying and I am praying. You are praying much more. There are nights when you pray the whole night. Other times you are praying for ten hours. Even tonight you can pray the whole night, but if you do not trust in Jesus' power, your prayer means nothing."

Kirit went into the little makeshift bamboo room adjacent to their home and closed the door. He confessed to the Lord that he was not trusting in His power. He confessed that early on in his walk he was very strong in faith but his love had grown cold, and he had begun to doubt the promises of God. "Lord, I believe what You said in Your Word," he declared.

Kirit opened up the Scriptures and remembered the story at the beginning of Luke 14 where Jesus healed the man swollen with fluid. Suddenly at midnight, Kirit was strengthened. He rushed to void a great amount of fluid, and his body returned to its normal strength.

Kirit went to open the door and called for Tarumala.

"Yes," she replied. She hadn't been able to sleep with Kirit suffering so terribly.

"It's okay," Kirit said. "I'm alive. Come out and let us give thanks together." They bowed before the Lord and thanked Him for His healing.

Kirit was encouraged by seeing the power of God in his own life. Since that day, he has taken great heart and delight in praying for people who are sick, because he knows that Jesus is able to heal.

JESUS HEALS A DEMON-POSSESSED MAN

Kirit always dreamed of new ways to declare the Gospel throughout Tripura. He knew that God had called him, and he was determined to follow Christ in obedience by making disciples everywhere. In 1983, he formed a Gospel team of four which would travel all over the state of Tripura in order to preach the Gospel.

Typically the team would go once a month and conduct several days of evangelistic meetings in different places. Kirit would use some of his two hundred rupee monthly salary and the love offerings they received from the churches for the ministry.

On one occasion, they went south. After preaching one night in one of the villages, a brother came running and warned Kirit to flee from that area with his team. It was already 9:00, and it was too late to travel anywhere else. Kirit wondered what could be amiss.

The brother said, "You're in danger. There is a man, Borokmon, who has taken a long sword and is shouting, 'Kirit, I will finish him!'"

"How does he know my name?" Kirit wondered. "How long has he been deranged like this?"

"Two years."

Kirit realized it was demon possession. "Don't worry," Kirit assured him. "I will come tomorrow morning at 10:00 with my team."

"No, no, no, no! We cannot bind him. We have tried, but he just breaks the rope and then the door," the man said.

"Brother, do not worry. I will not die. Just bind him with the strongest rope you can find, and lock him inside a room so that he cannot go out."

After breakfast, the team walked about thirteen kilometres to the village. When they arrived, Kirit asked, "Where is Borokmon?"

"He's in that house over there," an onlooker said.

They went to the house and opened the door. Kirit looked in and saw that Borokmon was bending over.

Kirit said to the onlookers, "Those who have faith in Jesus Christ, remain here. Those who don't, please go out."

Villagers had gathered, because they knew that Borokmon was demon possessed and wanted to see what would happen. Half the people left after Kirit's instruction.

Kirit had already trained his team. "Be strong in the Lord. He is going to do wonderful things for His glory." He then instructed some of them to loosen the ropes.

Kirit said to Borokmon, "Look at me. Tell me, what is your name?"

"Borokmon," the man quietly answered.

"Do you know me?" Kirit asked. Borokmon remained quiet. "Look at me," Kirit instructed him, but he didn't look.

"Let us be strong in the Lord. The Lord is with us. Let us pray," Kirit instructed his team.

Before they entered the house, Kirit had collected information about what kind of gods and goddesses were worshipped there. The people in that village especially revered the Hindu goddess Kali.

After praying together, Kirit then said, "In the name of Jesus of Nazareth, I command you to come out of him."

Borokmon fell down. Those with him asked, "What happened?"

"Don't worry," Kirit said. "He will be okay."

Kirit then gave him a Bible and a song book and he took it.

"So, Borokmon... tell me now, what happened?" Kirit asked.

Borokmon looked around nervously and said, "I am looking for Kali. She has long hair and a long tongue. She stands behind me all the time and tells me what to do and what not to do. Do you see her?"

"No," Kirit replied.

"Look over there, or out front. Or even out back... is she there?"

Kirit could tell that Borokmon was still fearful.

"She is gone now," Kirit assured him. "Believe in Jesus Christ, my friend. He is the one who has freed you."

The villagers heard what had happened and gathered around. They were very surprised and said, "Your Jesus is so powerful."

Kirit and his team stayed there that night and shared Christ's truth with the villagers. Some of the villagers believed and were baptized.

Afterward, Kirit took Borokmon with him to several other villages to testify about what God had done for him. Kirit then encouraged Borokmon to remain strong in the Lord and sent him back to continue to serve the Lord in his home village.

Later that year, a church was established there.

PART FIVE: CALCUTTA BIBLE COLLEGE

Global Outreach had a Bengali radio program ministry that was broadcast into a number of regions, including the state of Tripura. In May 1985, Sekhar was sent from Kolkata to follow up on individuals who had written to the program with questions and comments. He went to the large Baptist organization that Kirit worked with to look for a guide to accompany him to the various respondents throughout the state.

A senior leader of this group, Pastor Jong, introduced Sekhar to Kirit. Because Kirit was one of their missionaries, Jong asked him to take Sekhar around the state on his follow-up mission.

Sekhar had a list of names and addresses that kept him and Kirit busy for a month of ministry. After the two had finished, they returned to Kirit's birth town to debrief their time together before Sekhar's return to Kolkata. In the course of their discussion, Sekhar proposed that Kirit come to Kolkata to study at a well-known Bible college there. He suggested that his group would sponsor his studies.

Kirit had no interest in attending a Bible school—he just wanted to do ministry. He remembered the eighteen months in the seventies when he had worked in the bookshop of the Agartala mission compound while he was not travelling around Tripura doing his itinerant ministry. While he was there, he would take the opportunity to read the books in the shop, and Kirit thought that he had learned enough from that experience. He saw Bible school as unnecessary for a fruitful ministry.

Nevertheless, Kirit discussed the opportunity with Tarumala. She thought it was a good idea and advised him to take advantage of the open door. This meant that she would be responsible for their three children on her own for four years while he was away in Kolkata. Her rationale was that she had a small income from teaching which would be enough to take care of the children. She also felt that it was the right time, because the children were still young.

In the mid-eighties, Kirit travelled to Kolkata and arrived at the Bible college campus. He immediately sought out Sekhar, who took him to see Pastor Lloyd, the local director of the sponsoring group. The director, a Canadian, was also the pastor of Carey Baptist Church and the chairman of the college's board of directors, in addition to teaching music there. He served with his wife, Hazel, in the heart of Kolkata.

It was clear that Sekhar had already spoken to Pastor Lloyd about Kirit coming to study at the college. Pastor Lloyd quickly agreed to sponsor his studies, and he was welcomed on campus as a freshman.

Though Kirit arrived two months late, he took the challenge to catch up with what he had missed and kept a positive attitude in the midst of this hard work.

Kirit meets Hazel (Pastor Lloyd's widow) in Canada

CHURCH PLANTING AND OPPORTUNITIES

On Sunday mornings and evenings, the Bible college's students were required to be a part of ministry in the various churches connected to the college. For Kirit, this left time to add one more activity between 1:00 and 4:00 p.m.: church planting.

While in Kolkata, Kirit sought out others who were from his tribe. There were a number of Borok in the city who had come to find work there and were able to secure regular employment. In his second year at college, Kirit formed a Christian fellowship among the Borok in the southern quarter of Kolkata, and led it until he returned to Tripura.

One member of the Borok fellowship was a taxi driver for a television station. In his last year, Kirit asked him if he could schedule an appointment with a program director at the station so he could introduce himself.

Kirit arrived at the station, and a meeting was arranged with the assistant director. After introducing himself as a Tripuri student at the Bible college and chatting for a few minutes, he requested air time to present an Easter Sunday program. He asked if he and the college music team could present three or four songs.

Kirit noted that the songs would be presented in English because his college was an English medium school. The assistant director said that Kirit would have to speak with the station's English department head, then gave him directions to her office.

Kirit found her office and shared once again his desire to present a few Easter songs in English. The department head was very excited about the proposal. She told Kirit to bring the music team members to make a recording that would be aired the week before Easter.

He came back to the college to share the news with Pastor Lloyd. They quickly formed a music team and practiced continually.

Dr. John, principal of the college, was so elated by this opportunity that he asked Kirit, "Can you please allow me to speak just a few minutes during the television program?"

Kirit recommended, "We shouldn't be too pushy with this opportunity. They are, after all, allowing us to present several Easter songs. This is what they agreed to."

"Well then, can we have the name of our school appear on the screen at least?" John suggested.

It was interesting to have the principal requesting various things of Kirit, but the two had developed a tight-knit relationship during Kirit's studies, characterized by much mutual respect.

Kirit thought John's idea was prudent. One week later the team came to the station and recorded their four songs for the program. On the board behind where they were performing Kirit had written, "Music Team" and the name of his college.

Not only did the program air, but the station provided the music team an honorarium in the amount of 2,300 Indian rupees. It was a lot of money in Kolkata at the time, and the cheque was written in Kirit's name. He had to open a personal bank account in Kolkata—something he previously did not have—in order to cash the cheque. The music team each received a small amount, and they put the remaining money toward the college fund.

CONFLICT AND ENCOURAGEMENT

Kirit had already learned that relationships are complex through his ministry in Tripura. Where God is working, Satan is also very active. Kirit had become convinced that unless one was standing strong in the Lord, it would be easy to get caught up in the many conflicts that would inevitably come.

At Kirit's college, it eventually became obvious that there was a conflict between Dr. John, the principal, and one of the faculty members. Kirit was very close with the principal, and came to his home one day to find out what was bothering him.

"I am really disappointed with these people, this one family," John shared with Kirit.

Kirit asked him, "What happened?"

"There are so many things. This family does not like to respect or honour me as principal. They mock me and laugh at me."

Kirit listened as John shared with him. After a while, Kirit offered one piece of advice. He humbly said, "Uncle... just believe that the Holy Spirit is with you, and that He will work all things out for good."

Dr. John was encouraged. He knew that he simply needed to trust the Lord to be his defense, no matter what challenges he faced.

Kirit saw ministry not only as reaching out beyond the walls of the church, but also building up those around him.

SICKNESS

In 1988, Kirit became quite sick with boils. He informed Pastor Lloyd that due to his condition, he would be unable to study. The pastor told him that he should return home and recover before returning to complete his studies. Kirit didn't want to leave Kolkata and his studies. He nevertheless agreed because a spiritual authority figure had instructed him to do so.

Kirit ended up staying in Tripura for eight months, and missed his entire fourth year of studies at Bible college. He returned to Kolkata in June to complete his final year. Upon returning, he joined in with the group of students who had previously been junior to him, but were now his classmates.

TROUBLED

One day, Kirit was very troubled with worry about his father's eternal state. He wondered if he would see him in heaven or not, worried primarily that his father had not taken water baptism. He began to fast and pray, hoping to get an answer about this matter.

As Kirit prayed, he remembered the Word in John 3:16 that says that *"whoever believes in him shall not perish but have eternal life"* (NIV). He knew that his father had confessed faith in Jesus. Could he be in heaven without being baptized?

Kirit needed to grow in his theology. He remembered that it is by grace that we are saved, and not by any work that we perform. The message from Oswald Smith he'd read early in his Christian walk encouraged him once again.

Kirit also remembered the story of the thief on the cross beside Jesus. He was saved, but not baptized before his death. Kirit grew in his understanding of the Scriptures, and in the grace of God.

QUESTIONS

As Kirit studied the Scriptures, he increasingly rejoiced that God had chosen him. What a privilege to be a child of the King of Kings, after so many centuries of his people never hearing the Gospel message! Over the course of about 1,500 years, until 1947, the Borok people had been ruled by 184 different monarchs. Due to Indian influence, one of the kings had adopted the Hindu religion for all of the people.

New Zealand Baptist missionaries entered Tripura in 1938; however, the king forbade the missionaries to reach out to the Borok people. They were only allowed to work among the other minority tribal groups of the state. When the monarchy ended in 1947, with Tripura foregoing its independence and joining the nation-state of India, the door opened for the Gospel to go out among the Borok people.

Kirit was so grateful to be one of the first few believers among the Borok to accept the gift of life in Jesus Christ. His heart was full of hope for Christ to become known among his people. Several experiences in Kolkata, however, puzzled him.

Bible college students regularly engaged in evangelism on Saturdays. One day Kirit was walking around and noticed three Americans who stood out because of their white skin. What surprised Kirit about these young people was not that they were in Kolkata, but that they dressed like Hindus and were sitting on the side of the street playing drums and chanting.

Kirit was baffled. He approached the group. "Excuse me, brother—may I speak with you?" he asked politely.

"Who are you?" one of them asked.

"I am a student from a local Bible college," he replied.

"And what would you like to say?" they wondered.

Kirit said to them, "I just wanted to ask—why are you doing these things? Are you from America?"

"Yes, we are Americans," they replied.

Kirit always kept tracts in his pocket and, because his college was an English medium school, he had some in English. He presented a tract to them.

"What is this?" one man asked. Once he realized what it was, he said, "No need to give it to us. Take it back. Jesus Christ? No way!" They handed it back to Kirit.

Kirit could not understand how Americans, with their history of Gospel witness, could possibly be Hindu.

PASSING IT ON

On many Sundays during his time in Kolkata, Kirit would preach in local Bengali churches because he spoke Bengali. The principal of his college, Dr. John, would make these arrangements for Kirit to speak.

Some of the churches that Kirit visited in Kolkata were massive in structure. Built by the British during the time of their colonial rule in India, some of these facilities had seating capacity for anywhere between five hundred and two thousand individuals. It was heartbreaking for Kirit to see only a handful of believers present in each of them. He knew that numbers did not necessarily determine the health of the congregation, but he wondered how so many of these church buildings could be so empty.

Following the service one Sunday, during the fellowship time held over tea, he humbly asked the pastor, "Who will be your successor in ministry?"

The pastor answered, "Kirit, you should know one thing. Young people aren't loyal. They have no sense of direction, just going here and there. You cannot trust them."

The conversation was brief, and Kirit had to think about how to further respond.

Several weeks later, Kirit returned to the church to speak again. Again, over tea, Kirit initiated a conversation.

Kirit engaging in conversation

"Pastor, I want to tell you one thing. I am young, like a son of yours. By the way, how old are you now?"

"Sixty-five," the pastor responded.

Kirit, emboldened to lovingly challenge the pastor, said to him, "You only have a short time left. Please pray and ask the Lord to provide a successor. Invest in him so that he can faithfully carry on the ministry."

It seemed to Kirit that the Bengali churches struggled with the idea of surrendering authority and passing on leadership. The Gospel was first proclaimed among the Bengalis nearly two hundred years earlier by the man considered *"the father of modern missions,"* William Carey. Even though the Gospel had been with the small Bengali church for such a long time, Kirit felt it hadn't grown and taken root because a vision for the future was lacking.

Several years after leaving Kolkata, word came to Kirit that the pastor of this congregation had died. His church struggled to keep its doors open, and was eventually added to the list of stagnant fellowships in Kolkata.

Early in Kirit's ministry, he did not have the vision to make successors in ministry. Witnessing the state of the church among the Bengalis in West Bengal, however, gave him pause, and he began to see the necessity of intentionally working to establish leaders to carry on the ministry in the next generation.

Kirit observed that Jesus made disciples by taking them along with him as he ministered. Not only did Jesus provide lessons to the disciples, but he modelled faithfulness and obedience to them. Kirit determined to set an example in his speech, his preaching, and his prayer life. "Let my disciples learn from my example," Kirit thought.

Lying on his bed seven days before graduating, Kirit asked the Lord how he should go about passing on what he had learned during his four years of studies. Who should he teach? Then he realized that his wife should be his first student. This thought made him very excited—he knew it was what he should do.

He quickly went out and bought a Bengali Bible lesson book with one hundred studies for his wife, as she did not speak any English. "You will be my first student," Kirit told Tarumala when he returned to Tripura. Kirit was now prepared to pass on the things which he had learned.

PART SIX:
TRIPURA BAPTIST CHRISTIAN UNION (1991-2004)

FINANCIAL CRISES

Shortly before graduating from Bible college, Kirit received word that the New Zealand Baptist group was planning to terminate its financial support for the large Baptist group that employed him. The New Zealand Baptists had been instrumental in establishing the denomination in 1938, and had supported its ongoing work since Western missionaries were expelled from Tripura in 1972. Now, they transferred their support to concentrate on their work in Bangladesh instead.

Following his graduation in April 1990, Kirit returned to Tripura. He was immediately reappointed as a missionary following his five year absence. However, the denomination was now in the middle of a financial crisis.

The large mission group was made up of twelve different associations throughout Tripura. Kirit and Tarumala belonged to the southern association subgroup. After the New Zealand Baptists withdrew their support, there was a decision to decentralize oversight, administration and care for the affiliated associations. This meant that each association became independent financially and received limited administrative help from the denomination offices. Ten of the twelve associations faced financial hardship due to the changes which took place. Kirit and Tarumala's group was one of those which struggled.

In May 1990, the members of their subgroup gathered to appoint a new secretary. Several members were nominated for the position, but none were willing to consider filling the post. Being the secretary would mean bearing a great burden, particularly in the middle of a financial crisis.

When the New Zealand Baptists withdrew their support, the association was not even close to reaching its budget for supporting the pastors and evangelists of the group, let alone the fees designated for the larger denomination. Their smaller denomination was receiving approximately 20,000 rupees in tithes at the time of the decentralization. This was only a fraction of what was needed to cover the budget for staff support, which was 74,000 rupees. Becoming secretary at this time would be a huge responsibility.

Finally, a nomination came that Kirit be secretary. He could see that no one else was willing. When he accepted, he immediately knew that he would need to lead in the area of stewardship.

Kirit got right down to work and initiated an intense program among the seventeen member churches. He began calling the churches to pray fervently for the Lord's provision. Each week he would visit two or three congregations, and spend two days with them—fasting, praying, and studying the Scriptures. The two day gathering would conclude with an all-night prayer meeting. He did this with each of the churches, and then began to repeat the cycle once he had visited each one. It was an intense year of ministry as the churches cried out to God that He meet their need.

It was a very challenging season for everyone. The association was not able to pay the pastors and evangelists their meagre salaries. Kirit and Tarumala had to do without remuneration for seven months during that year. Despite the very real struggle, they kept on trusting the Lord.

The audit results for the association published after Kirit had served for a year became a testimony of the Lord's provision. Only then was it realized that a total of 75,000 rupees had been collected in offerings during the previous year. The amount was just enough to cover the budget of 74,000 rupees for the salaries of the pastors and evangelists. Believers rejoiced as they witnessed the grace of God among them.

The executive of the larger state association took note of Kirit's leadership, and called on him in 1995. An orange crop failure in the Jampui Hills of the North Tripura district was causing great distress. The executive asked Kirit if he could go to minister in the suffering churches. For a number of years, the financial health of these churches had been in decline, and their dependence on the orange harvest was on full display when the crop failed.

The churches in Jampui Hills were older than most in the province, as the Gospel had come to that area much earlier than in other parts of Tripura. When Kirit visited, he discovered that these churches had grown complacent in the Lord.

He spent just over two weeks there, and visited each of the ten churches in that region. Kirit shared a challenge from the Word of God—that they bring their offerings as a sign of gratitude for His grace, even in the midst of their financial hardship. The believers began to weep and bring their offerings to the Lord.

Following the ministry tour, the state government stepped in and initiated a program to help farmers plant coffee as an alternative crop. The believers were thankful for this opportunity, and saw this as God's grace toward them in their need.

While the local association raised enough resources in 1990–1991 for its own staff, the state denomination headquarters also required resources from each of the associations for their ongoing operations. Finally, in 1998, Kirit's group was able to meet both their own budget and the prescribed denomination fees due to the state association. Kirit resigned from the post of secretary in 1999, after leading the association through the challenging years. When Kirit stepped down, it was not difficult for the local association to find a member to assume his post. It was no longer in a financial crisis.

God was not only at work in the churches of the local association providing for their financial needs; more importantly, He was building His church in Tripura. Between 1990 and 1999, forty new churches with twenty to seventy members each were planted through the ministry of this group.

DISCOURAGEMENT

Even though he had much evidence of God's grace, there were several times when Kirit became very discouraged in the ministry, and considered a change in career. His charismatic personality and strong leadership skills frequently resulted in offers from political parties to be their leader.

One of the most significant temptations came in the mid-nineties, when Kirit had become particularly unhappy. Amidst personal financial hardship, Kirit was remembering the many challenges he had faced in the ministry up until that point. He remembered how his life had been threatened multiple times, and was thinking that the ministry might simply be too risky to continue. Perhaps it would be better to leave? Kirit began to doubt his call.

In the midst of his melancholy, the political assembly election was approaching, and a group of political leaders approached him.

"Brother," they persuasively told Kirit, "no one respects you for this church work. This is such a meagre ministry. You are actually a very competent man, and you can be a government minister and become rich if you join with us."

Kirit was very tempted. His discouragement and the financial pressure fed the allure of the offer.

He did not share his thoughts with Tarumala. However, these conversations with the political leaders were not unknown to her. The delegations visited Kirit on a number of occasions, and his wife served them tea as they talked. Not only did she watch and listen to the conversations closely, but she read Kirit like a book.

"So," Tarumala asked him one day, "are you going to become a politician?"

"Yes," Kirit responded. "This is actually good for you and for us." He continued, "Your salary as a public school teacher is very small and we need more money in order to put our children in a better school. They need better opportunities. And we do not even have a house now. We are just living in a rented place, and we may not have enough money to pay our rent at the end of the month. They will tell us to get out and we will have nowhere to go."

Kirit and Tarumala had decided to move from his birth town to another place a year earlier, because there was no high school in the village where they had lived. The children were growing, and they were trying to ensure that they got the necessary education.

Tarumala was short with Kirit. "If you want to get involved in politics, then you go and stay in Agartala and do that." She was not willing to live with Kirit if he was going to pursue that path. Her father had, and she knew how it had negatively influenced her family.

Kirit knew he had a decision to make—but how? There were so many considerations. He was still leaning toward politics because the grass looked so green to him on that side.

One evening, everything changed. Kirit was reading Scripture and praying. He came to Matthew chapter 28, and the Lord spoke mightily to him. He read that Jesus held all authority in heaven and on earth. It was not that Kirit had never read those words before, but the reality of Jesus' supreme authority over all came to him like a flash of lightning and captivated his heart. Yes, he had read it correctly: Jesus held *all* authority. Kirit was strengthened in his spirit.

He continued reading the passage, including Jesus' promise that he would be present with his disciples until the very end of the age. The peace of knowing that the Lord of the universe promised his enduring presence flooded Kirit's thoughts and gripped him. How could he neglect so great a promise? How could he be so overwhelmed by these current pressures and challenges when he knew this promise was true?

Kirit humbled himself before the Lord, and repented for seeking security in anything other than Him. Kirit was resolute. He would forsake all, and continue in the ministry to which God called him.

SURRENDERING ALL TO JESUS

The following day Kirit approached Tarumala to talk.

"If we are going to continue in the Lord's ministry, we need to trust Him," Kirit told Tarumala.

She was excited to hear that Kirit wanted to continue serving Jesus. Tarumala always opposed any suggestion which deviated from this focus, and delighted in persevering in the work of God.

Kirit continued, "We do have needs, but God will provide. We need to be willing to surrender everything to Him. We don't have an office, or a mission compound. So what will we do?"

"I can sell the paddy land that I inherited from my father," Tarumala suggested.

A bit surprised by the offer, but at the same time very happy, Kirit agreed.

The next day, Tarumala went to visit her father. Even though he was not a Christian, he agreed to the plan because it was her land and she was free to do with it what she wanted.

Tarumala came back with 10,000 rupees.

Kirit also decided to sell his own property. After reconciliation with his father, he had been given a portion of a pineapple garden. Also, the couple had some land which they had purchased from Kirit's siblings as an investment. They sold all of their land, and proceeded to purchase a property that they could use for the ministry in the new town where they were living.

STARTING AN ENGLISH MEDIUM SCHOOL

There was interest in their new town to start an English medium school because of all the advantages that knowing English would provide for the children. Despite several attempts to open a school, nobody had succeeded in getting anything started. The villagers particularly wanted Kirit's involvement, because he was educated in English and could oversee such an initiative.

Kirit and Tarumala knew that an English school would be a great blessing to the community. Because the vast majority of the townspeople were Hindus, they envisioned the wonderful opportunity a school could provide for sharing the Gospel.

In June 1996, they commenced operations. At first, the school opened for ten students in a nursery school. Twelve students were added the second year, and it continued to grow.

At the 1997 annual meeting of the smaller southern association, which was held in their town, some individuals told Kirit and Tarumala that they should not be operating an English school. Several attendees argued that it should be handed over to others, considering it inappropriate for Kirit to run a school while serving as a missionary with them. He did not feel the need to respond to their arguments.

One week later, a representative was sent to talk with Kirit. The man knew Kirit well, and respected him as an elder in the ministry.

"Uncle," the man began, "to whom do you wish to hand over your school? Have you made a plan?" he asked directly.

"No," Kirit responded, "I'm not planning to hand it to over to anyone."

The man replied, "Why not? It was discussed at length at the annual meeting with hundreds of people last week."

Kirit spoke confidently, "You can discuss it with thousands and millions of people. That's not my concern. Before starting the school I prayed to the Lord, asking Him that through this school we would be able to reach the unreached. All these people are Hindus."

The representative was upset. "You heard what we discussed at the meeting and what we advised. We will take action if you don't respond properly!"

For the man who confronted Kirit, the matter remained unresolved. For Kirit, on the other hand, there was no question about continuing the school.

INTERNATIONAL OPPORTUNITIES

In December 1999, Kirit received an invitation to travel to Chittagong Hill Tracts in Bangladesh to participate in Awana Club training. While he was there, he took the opportunity to speak at a few churches and encourage the believers. He was invited back to speak at a three-day conference, focused on the second coming of Christ, in March 2000.

A few days after returning from speaking at the conference, several members of the local association approached Kirit and asked him, "Why, as one of our missionaries, did you not ask permission to go to Bangladesh?" Kirit replied to them, "I am very loyal and submissive to the association as my employer. However, this work is part of being faithful to God's call to go and make disciples of all nations. We should first and foremost obey the direction of our Lord." They continued to object and indicated that he was required to get permission from the association.

Kirit was astonished and puzzled. He wondered to himself, "How can I follow God's leading in this situation? If I had asked permission, it would not have been granted."

Kirit knew that the association would never permit him to go. He had notified them of his ministry plans in the past, but it was not sufficient for them. They wanted the Executive Committee to grant approval whenever Kirit went out of the country.

Kirit prayed to the Lord and asked Him what he should do next.

CONTINUED OPPOSITION & RESIGNATION FROM THE STATE ASSOCIATION

In November 2002, another invitation from Bangladesh came to Kirit. This time, Bangladeshi church leaders invited him to come and speak in different churches in the Comilla district, just over Tripura's western border with Bangladesh. Kirit believed that the Gospel was good news for all nations, not only for those in Tripura. He travelled for ten days in Bangladesh, ministering in the churches and encouraging them in mission.

Kirit also began to teach and encourage believers in some non-Baptist organizations that were emerging in Tripura. A

Presbyterian group had invited Kirit to provide some teaching, to which he heartily agreed. Again the local association came to Kirit to criticize him for his choices.

They argued, "As a Baptist pastor and leader, you should not go to help other organizations."

Kirit replied simply, "I am very sorry about the trouble that this is causing."

One pastor spoke up adamantly, "We too get invitations to speak to other groups, but we do not go. Why do you have the audacity to go yourself?"

Kirit could see that tension had been slowly growing between the association and him. The opposition he was facing within the group was proving to be a distraction from valuable Gospel ministry.

In February 2003, Kirit bought three computers for the English school. For the inaugural event using the computers at the school, Kirit invited the leaders of the local association to celebrate with them. This was indeed a significant event.

"You are building quite the property here," said the vice-president (Kirit was the president). "Tell us, how much are you working in the churches?"

He replied, "I prayed to the Lord and started working. This property was bought for the glory of God and so that His Gospel will be proclaimed. It is not for my personal purpose."

A week later, the association head called for Kirit to come and meet him in Agartala.

When Kirit arrived, he was told that he needed to close the school immediately. They argued that he would never be able to serve the church well because he would be preoccupied with the affairs of the school.

Kirit perceived their jealousy, and did not respond to their comments or directives.

In May 2004, the state organization held its annual general meeting. During the meeting Kirit was nominated to be president. Several leaders from his local association were agitated by this nomination, and opposed Kirit. They were jealous that somebody who used to be such a poor man was now operating a school with computers. One of them voiced a concern about whether or not he could care for the church, claiming again that the school would be a hindrance to his service.

One of the church members spoke up in response and said, "Since Kirit and Tarumala opened the school, Kirit has not stopped visiting the churches. We have not even seen him one day in the school teaching a class."

In response to the witness, there was only silence.

Kirit was elected president. The local opposition, however, continued unabated.

Just a few months later, on August 19, 2004, Kirit resigned from the state organization. He had tolerated all the opposition which he had been facing from within the denomination, but eventually the divisiveness became such that Kirit did not see his continued involvement with them as profitable for the Kingdom of God. So, he discussed resigning with Tarumala, and she fully supported his decision. Her only caveat was that Kirit continue in the Lord's ministry, which was something he was determined to do.

Immediately in response, a two-man commission came from the head office. They told Kirit to withdraw his resignation and return to his leadership of their group.

They asked him, "Why did you resign? We just elected you president. How are you not satisfied with that?"

"It is not a matter of being satisfied with my position," Kirit said. "Whenever I go and respond to God's call, *you* are the ones who are not satisfied. Therefore, I believe that I should not disturb you."

Kirit relayed the various oppositions that he had been facing in the ministry from both the local and state organizations. He told them about the disapproval directed at him for operating an English school, while no one mentioned the fact that twelve families in the community had accepted Christ through the school's ministry. "I believe it is better for me now to simply go and serve the Lord freely on my own."

After hearing these things, the delegation suggested that they pray about his continuation as denomination president. Kirit, however, was firm in his decision to leave them and continue in the Lord's work independently.

The representatives were surprised at Kirit's resolve. "Without us, you will definitely not have any ministry success," they suggested. "Who will support you? Who will provide money for the ministry?"

Kirit was saddened. He responded humbly, "If God does not want to bless me in the ministry, I have no problem with that. Jesus himself called and saved me in 1972 when I was absolutely helpless. He has been faithful all this time. No matter what I need, please do not be worried for me."

Kirit knew that his wife was also very strong in faith, trusting in the promises of God, and that they had no need to be concerned about how the Lord would provide. Even though the delegates tried to create doubt so he would rescind his resignation, Kirit remained steadfast in his trust in Jesus.

The commission did not know how to respond. They were losing a strong, faithful leader. Finally, they left Kirit an invitation to continue with them as they went on their way.

Following the attempt to change Kirit's mind, the organization circulated a letter among all their churches indicating that he and Tarumala were no longer members and that they should not associate with them in any way.

The secret letter soon came into Kirit's hands. A friend supplied a copy for him to see.

Kirit was not surprised. In fact, he did not even take offense. He was aware of the struggles in the church in Tripura, and that believers often demonstrate that they are controlled by jealousy and not by the Holy Spirit.

Kirit had his confidence in the fact that his name was written in the Lamb's book of life. He was a member of Christ's kingdom, not a member of the state association's kingdom.

The denomination's leaders began to observe how the Lord was blessing Kirit and Tarumala's ministry following his resignation. They came to Kirit and asked him, "From where did you get money to do these different things?"

"What you need to understand is that this is God's ministry," Kirit informed them. "He is the provider. The Lord has brought people into our lives to walk with us."

The group did not officially seek reconciliation with Kirit, but two years after his resignation, members began to invite Kirit to speak in their churches. The leadership also began to warm up to him again.

PART SEVEN: ESTABLISHING HUMAN CARE MISSION

Kirit sharing memories with old friends

Kirit and Tarumala registered their mission as a non-governmental organization (NGO). They established this NGO in order to have an appropriate framework from which to operate some of their work, such as the English school. Now that they were independent from the denomination, this NGO was a necessary blessing to continue carrying out their ministry.

The focus of the ministry has been entirely on making Jesus known to those who do not yet know him. All the activities which they have initiated and continued have been evaluated on their impact for the church planting ministry.

BIBLE TRAINING PROGRAMS

Remembering the vision with which he had left his college when he graduated, Kirit determined to focus his ministry efforts on being a disciple-maker. Shortly after leaving the state organization, Kirit began running a one-year Bible school from the mission compound in his new town. Some students would come from different parts of Tripura and live in the humble hostel prepared for them; others would come as day scholars from the community and return to their homes for the evenings and weekends.

The ministry has trained over three hundred students at its Bible college over the years. Some of the graduates of the one-year program have gone on to further studies at different Bible colleges in India which offer full Bachelor's degrees. Many have gone on to serve the Lord in other missions and organizations. Kirit is delighted to see them trained up and working in the service of the Lord, whether or not they continue with his mission.

Kirit also implemented an evening Bible class in February 2006 in Agartala city. The one-year course runs Saturday and Sunday evenings. Kirit has been training professionals, and even evangelists and pastors from different organizations and denominations who are not able to attend seminary or Bible training elsewhere.

CHURCH PLANTING

The key focus of all the Bible training has been to prepare leaders to go throughout Tripura to make disciples and plant new churches where there are none. Kirit has enlisted a number of missionaries and evangelists who have graduated from their training to be in the full-time ministry with his mission, as funds allow. Missionaries are sent to various areas of the state to share the Gospel with the unreached. Commonly, Kirit will appoint at least two missionaries in one location so that they have fellowship with each other and can work together.

The group of missionaries serving under Kirit's leadership gets together once every month to do mobile evangelism together. One of the appointed missionaries will make arrangements in their area, or even in a new area where they are not yet working, and arrange for the team to travel together in order to share the Gospel in those places.

Kirit is not interested in building the kingdom of his mission. Often when the missionary team does mobile evangelism and fruit is borne from the work, they will encourage the new believers to connect with a church family in the area. Most commonly, the churches that they are plugged into are different denominations.

BENGALI VISION

Following the partition of British India in 1947 and the merger of Tripura with the Indian Union in 1949, there was a significant influx of Bengali migrants into Tripura. The partition was based on religious lines, and many Hindu Bengalis left Bangladesh (formerly East Pakistan) because the population there was predominantly Muslim. In 1971, when Bangladesh fought for independence from Pakistan, the migration intensified. Operation World (2010) notes that before these events, 85% of the population in Tripura were indigenous; as of 2010, they made up less than 28%.[31]

---

31 Mandryk, *Operation World*.

These drastic population changes have been the source of significant hostility between the new Bengali majority and the indigenous Tripura peoples. Ethnic tensions boiled over and fuelled the communal riots of 1980. The political and economic power of the state has been taken over by the unwelcome immigrants. Hatred lingers between the indigenous people and the Bengalis.

Kirit, too, used to hate the Bengalis. One day, however, as Kirit spent time in Scripture, he was reading Jesus' words in Luke 6:27–28, *"Pray for your enemy. Love your enemy. Don't curse them but bless them"* (paraphrased). The Spirit of God spoke to Kirit through His Word in that moment. This scriptural diagnostic examination of his heart showed Kirit that his attitude toward Bengalis was not right. Bitterness and malice, no matter how seemingly justified, were not characteristic of being a child of the Most High. Kirit repented of his hatred.

The pride of the Borok people became evident to Kirit through this word from God. He could see how the Bengalis had been sent by God to humble the indigenous peoples, who had become extremely hopeless over the last seventy years as a result. He realized that this hopelessness had been the great engine for so many to come to Christ—they saw their need for the Gospel in the midst of weakness.

Kirit began to pray about how he could reach the Bengalis with the Gospel. He tried a few things, but did not have any success. Then, as he was praying in October 2008, he thought of a way to gather a large group of Bengalis.

He was travelling to a conference in Maharashtra at the time, and shared his burden and plan with a friend. He told him that the Bengalis always enjoy "parties," and that he was planning to hold a "Pre-Christmas Party" in the capital city. He wanted to serve sweets, always a lure for Bengalis.

The friend asked him, "How much will you need for all this?"

Kirit told him his budget and said, "I will also need 5,000 Bengali New Testaments for distribution."

Someone at the conference committed to providing the sweets and refreshments.

Kirit was encouraged.

On his way back to Tripura, when he travelled through Kolkata, he met with his former Bible college principal, Dr. John. He shared the vision with him, too. Dr. John immediately agreed to provide the Bengali New Testaments for the ministry.

The event was approaching quickly, and Kirit wondered what else could be done to attract more people. A bold solution came to mind. Kirit had an idea that if he could get the state's Chief Minister to attend as an honorary guest, then Hindu Bengalis would be interested in attending the meeting. He humbly presented his request, and it was accepted. God had given Kirit favour.

When word got out about a "Christmas Party" that the Chief Minister would attend, interest in the event grew. On the day of the party, Kirit watched the venue fill to its capacity (about eight hundred people) and thanked the Lord for His favour.

A Christmas program was presented. Kirit stood to present the key address. He presented the hope of salvation found only in Jesus Christ, and appealed to everyone to repent and believe.

As was the custom, the honorary guest was invited to make a few remarks at the end of the service. The Chief Minister thanked Kirit for inviting him to his first Christmas party, and mentioned that he had made an interesting appeal to the people. Sensing the Holy Spirit giving him boldness, in front of the whole crowd Kirit told the Minister that he, too, needed to be born again. The Minister did not make a decision that day, but asked to be invited to any future party that Kirit would organize.

However, fourteen Bengalis did respond to the message that day. Shortly after the event, they were all baptized, and a new church fellowship began in Agartala.

Today, Kirit calls the Borok believers in Tripura to pray for Bengalis, but he continues to face resistance. Most Christian leaders in Tripura are opposed to doing ministry among the Bengalis. "The more we love them, the more they betray us," they say.

The general attitude of the Borok leaders is that there is work to do among their own people, and they should focus their energies there. Kirit, however, hopes to see a burden to reach all peoples with the Gospel emerge from the believers in Tripura.

WORKING FOR RELIGIOUS FREEDOMS IN TRIPURA

Kirit has welcomed a unique opportunity to work with all the churches in Tripura. An interdenominational body was formed about a decade ago to advocate for human rights and religious freedom in the state. A key impetus for forming this coalition was that Christians were forced to participate in various Hindu festivals against their will. Money for Hindu temples and idols would be demanded of them, and they had no legal option to avoid the pressures. This forum was formed in order to present a united appeal to the government for their grievances.

Kirit was elected president of this new group when the post became vacant after several years, and was re-elected by the interdenominational body for a second three-year term. After Kirit had begun to serve as president, he led a delegation to meet with the chief secretary of the State of Tripura on the matter of Christians being confronted by Hindus to contribute to their activities.

The secretary's response was to circulate a letter to all the police superintendents throughout the state, ordering that Christians should not be forced to give to Hindu causes. It was a great relief for all the believers throughout Tripura.

But Kirit was not satisfied to have the forum limit itself to Christian grievances in Tripura. He longed to see believers across denominations united in Gospel mission. Conflict and jealousy between church leaders is all too common. In fact, two pastors who had a clash not far from his birth town actually physically fought each other, and both were hospitalized as a result. The testimony to those outside the church is terrible. Kirit knows that the Church needs to be characterized by love for one another if it wants to be effective in reaching the lost.

When Kirit introduced the idea that the forum hold an interdenominational meeting, the immediate response was "Who will pay for such a gathering?" No group was interested in financing such a project. Kirit wondered how each denomination and mission had resources to pay for its own meetings, but did not have resources for a meeting from which those outside their group would benefit. This was a great sadness for Kirit, illustrating how people desired to build their own kingdom much more than sacrificially serving for the Kingdom of Christ.

GOSPEL BOOKLET DISTRIBUTION

Kirit made a contact in central India with a ministry that provided booklets in various languages containing a Gospel presentation in cartoon format. It was a thrilling offer for Kirit, because this ministry was able to provide the booklets completely free of charge.

Beginning in 2015, Kirit commissioned a two-man team to coordinate this massive project. Their job was to travel to the various districts of Tripura and make "sub-partners" with churches who would be willing to distribute these Gospel booklets in their region. Once the sub-partners were registered and in agreement, the mission in central India would ship the Gospel booklets directly to them in their locations in the chosen districts of Tripura. The first year of the initiative, 250,000 booklets were distributed. The majority were in the Bengali language, and some were in English as well. In 2016, a total of 378,000 were distributed in other parts of Tripura. Kirit's team was eager to continue expanding the program; however, the ministry in central India was not able to provide the planned number of 500,000 booklets in 2017. They were only able to distribute 375,000. There are 548,000 to be distributed in 2018. After another campaign in 2019, the last three districts in Tripura will have been reached.

Kirit's vision is that all the people in Tripura would hear the Gospel message by 2020. With a population of four million in the state, the Gospel booklet distribution campaign has contributed significantly to the realization of this vision. Additionally, his organization has implemented a follow-up ministry, so that appropriate action can be taken where there is a positive response to the Gospel booklets.

Kirit remembers the prayer he offered early in his Christian life, when he asked the Lord not to take him home until half of his people had become believers. He is thankful for the opportunity of seeing the Gospel being made known to so many throughout Tripura.

PART EIGHT: PARTNERSHIP IN THE GOSPEL

A few years ago, Brother David, head of ENGAGE, visited Kirit and Tarumala in Tripura. Kishor, at that time a college principal but later a field advisor with an associated American charity, suggested that David visit Kirit and see the ministry that he was carrying out there. Kishor had attended Bible college with Kirit in the late 1980s, and they had maintained a little contact over the years. Kishor was aware that the ministry was bearing much fruit. Immediately upon visiting Kirit, Brother David formed a special bond with him. They had a likeminded passion and vision for spreading the Gospel and planting new churches. David returned to Canada following his two-month tour in Asia, and strongly recommended that his mission form a ministry partnership with Kirit's ministry in India.

The Canadian charity began supporting seven missionaries with Kirit's mission in the middle of 2012. Kirit was delighted by this support because it enabled them to do even more. Prior to this support, he had sent out several missionaries as local support allowed. Once the Canadians began their partnership, Kirit's mission continued to do what it could, and Kirit encouraged the churches to do even more. He is a firm believer in churches being active in mission themselves. His vision is to see all his churches be multiplying congregations.

In each subsequent year, a team has been sent from Canada to work with Kirit. A particular focus has been coordinating leadership seminars. Kirit has brought together leaders from within the churches connected to his mission on several occasions.

Recently, the Canadians worked with Kirit to coordinate a conference with the interdenominational human rights forum. Kirit hoped to focus on unity around the Gospel among the different denominations, and also highlight the need to reach the Bengali people. The Canadian speakers addressed these topics in their messages. Delegates from ten of the eighteen major denominations in Tripura gathered in Agartala for the conference. However, at least one denomination which had an unresolved conflict with the large state organization did not send any representatives because the event was being held at its mission compound.

The hesitation of several groups to participate in the conference highlighted the need to continue to work toward unity.

VISITING CANADA

Kirit visiting friends in Canada

Some years ago, Kirit visited Canada for about three weeks. Brother David had invited Kirit to connect with churches in three provinces so that people could begin to get to know him. One of the charity's objectives is to have Canadians personally know its partners, like Kirit.

Kirit enjoyed meeting many of David's friends, and invited many believers to visit their ministry back in India. Commonly, when hearing the invitation, people would respond by saying that they would pray about it. Kirit, in his typical jovial manner, would respond, "No need to pray. God has already made it clear in His Word that we are to go to the nations."

He again visited Canada two years later in order to further some of the relationships he had built, and share more broadly what God is doing in Tripura.

BIBLES FOR TRIPURA

When the Canadian charity's team travelled to Kirit and Tarumala's district in northern Tripura, they visited a rural congregation there. It was a church planted by one of the missionaries under Kirit's leadership. The believers of the church were from the Borok people, and the team asked how many of them owned a whole Bible in their own language. Only one person in the fellowship had a complete Bible in the Kok Borok language.

Kirit had mentioned the need among his people for Bibles. The Scriptures had been translated into Kok Borok, but there had never been a significant printing of them. He had a burden to see that change. Canadian friends began raising some of the resources necessary to help fund the project.

Several years ago, Kirit decided to put in an order for Bibles to the Bible Society in Kolkata. He did not have the funds available for the project, but decided to bear the burden if necessary. His plan was to sell the Bibles at a reasonable price to those who could afford it, and to give other copies away to those who could not. Any profit from selling the Bibles, it was decided, would go toward further printing and distribution.

In early January 2018, nearly six months after the target date to have the Bibles delivered in Tripura, 3009 Kok Borok Bibles were delivered for the glory of God. Generous friends in Canada provided about two-thirds of the needed cost of the Bibles.

GROWTH OF THE CHURCH

The Lord Jesus has been at work mightily over the last forty-five years in Tripura. When Kirit became a Christian in the early 1970s, there may have only been about fifty believers among the Borok people. Today, according to Kirit, it is estimated that approximately 175,000 are believers,[32] out of a total of 1.2. million Borok. Kirit's dream is to see the remaining unreached hear the Gospel and have an opportunity to respond to it. Although God has used him mightily to bring in a great harvest, he knows partnership is needed to continue to make Christ known.

Our prayer is that together we can see a great harvest of souls in Tripura. And we pray not only that at least 50% of the Borok people would name Christ as their Saviour and Lord (as Kirit prays to happen before the Lord takes him home), but that there would be a great harvest among the Bengalis as well.

To God be the glory. Amen.

---

32 Figures in *Operation World* (2010) by Jason Mandryk and the Joshua Project (joshuaproject.net) would suggest that this estimate is quite accurate.

CONCLUDING REMARKS
BY THE COMPILER

As you read these stories, I hope that they raised some thoughts about how God works in the world. I thought of calling this section, *Mission Dilemmas: What Would You Do?* But maybe, it is really just about reflecting on God's work.

So, in the story of Philemon, did you think about how challenging it would be to consider going back to your country in a time when your faith was very unwelcome? And with young children! Did you realize how much the opportunities in media were miracles in that country, and beyond logical possibility for that time—unplanned for, but entered into with faith and much prayer? And what does it take to encourage others in their work, even while your own work is often challenging, and when your own resources are always being stretched?

When you read about Dhan, did you realize how difficult it would be to receive specialized training while raising a family? Did you consider the choices he needed to make—first of all early in his ministry, and then again as he established a new work? And think of the impact of his work for Philemon, as well as what it would have felt like for Philemon to lose Dhan to his own ministry, yet to have mentored him to be able to do this successfully? Dhan's wife is also preparing for further ministry, while being of great help to the follow-up work of Philemon's media ministries.

When you read about Habil, did you feel that you had gone back a century—to a time when everything was done by walking in frontier areas? And in that setting, how would you deal with constant floods, rains, and a major earthquake? All the foreign resources were put to work around the major cities, but in the mountains, there was much less to work with and it wasn't time-ly. How can one trust God in those circumstances and deal with their lingering effects? Over 80% of the one hundred churches in that area were destroyed or made unsafe by the earthquakes in 2015, and many houses were also destroyed. In our records, we find any aid sent to this area is always split between Christians and non-believers, so that there is no question of Habil's love for all.

In the story of Kirit, what did you learn about this former monarchy that joined India about the same time Newfoundland joined Canada? What did you think about how Kirit's commitment to his Lord was tested? Did you think about how important it is to have the Word in your own language? How would you have approached the Bengali people as many migrated into your homeland and became the majority? How has Kirit inspired you to think of what you could do in your own province to say "Yes!" to Jesus?

I trust you will find your curiosity leading you to think about some of these things. I also hope that you will find yourself drawn to prayer—that in this way, you will come alongside these people, and many more of our fellow believers around the globe. And you are invited to ask us more about other leaders ENGAGE is coming alongside of in our work around the world.

Thank you so much for reading about these leaders whom God has blessed, and for taking the opportunity to come alongside them!

—Brother Bruce

APPENDIX ONE

PREM PRADHAN'S STORY:

"I KNOW A MAN WHO DIED AND ROSE AGAIN"[33]

In order to allow the reader to get a feel of the work of God over time in Nepal, we add this further article on Prem, published by another mission. In Prem's time, a handful of believers came to Christ and were sold out evangelists; they paid with prison terms so they could live their faith publically. The results we see today are largely due to the faithfulness of these men over half a century ago.

Prem Pradhan took the Bible and told the street preacher he would read it. The preacher had studied with Bahkt Singh, a renowned Bible teacher in India who taught his disciples the Word of God line by line, precept by precept.

Born in Nepal, Prem had never heard of Jesus. But because he served in the Indian army, he could freely consider reading the Scriptures. Prem read God's Word 12 times during the next few months.

After praying and giving his life to the Lord, Prem knew God wanted him to return to his own people in the Hindu kingdom of Nepal and tell them about the Man who died and rose again—the Man Jesus Christ.

"But, Lord," Prem said, "I can't. I have a lame leg." He had injured his leg during World War II. How could he trek through the Himalayas?

After three years, Prem surrendered and went home to share his faith. But his family rejected him.

---

33 Originally published as "I Know a Man Who Died and Rose Again," in *Establishing a Witness: Stories of Indigenous Missionaries Reaching the World for Christ* (Christian Aid Mission, 2018), 4–9.

He walked for a year in Nepal over mountains and through forests, fields, and rivers to find one disciple. He slept in barns, on back porch stoops, and under trees in the woods. He ate when someone offered him food.

"I know a Man who died and came to life again," Prem would say to people he encountered along his journey. Not many responded. No one believed.

FIRST CONVERSIONS

In the eleventh month of Prem's yearlong travel, he came to the house of a woman who had suffered paralysis for seven years. She had spent all she had on the Hindu Lama, but he could not make her walk. Prem told the woman and the Lama, who stood nearby, that he knew Jesus, who was powerful enough to heal her. "Then pray that He will heal me," the woman said.

A moment of doubt assailed Prem's faith. "Lord, what shall I do?" he inwardly prayed.

Prem knelt beside the woman's bed and, gently yet fervently, lifted his petition to the Lord. At the close of his prayer, he helped the woman place her legs over the bedside. Slowly, she leaned forward until her feet touched the floor. And then, she stood. She steadied herself and took a tiny step forward—and then another and another. She walked to the door and saw the mountains for the first time in seven years.

"Oh, look at those beautiful mountains!" she said.

The miracle stunned the handful of witnesses, and they all gave their lives to Jesus.

The Hindu Lama was stunned as well. "By what magic did you cause this woman to walk?" he asked.

"By no magic," Prem answered. "By the power of Jesus Christ."

The Lama believed.

PREM IN PRISON

In Nepal, it is against the law to change one's religion, but Prem openly baptized the new Christians. Believing that Christians should be able to publicly practice their faith, Prem even invited the village leaders to witness the baptism.

The authorities arrested them all and proceeded to interrogate the new Christians one by one.

They made no progress with the first believer they questioned. "Just say you're not a Christian, and we'll let you go," they told him. When he refused, they moved to the next one.

"The first person denied Christ," they told him. "You deny Christ, and we'll let you go, too."

But their deception failed to work on the second believer... or on the third or on the fourth. Every one of them maintained their faith.

The authorities threw them all into prison, sentencing those who were baptized for one year. Prem, who baptized them, was sentenced for six years.

Nine people crowded into a tiny cell with poor ventilation and no sanitation. Each received a cup of rice per day, uncooked, and a cup of water. They slept in the stench on stone floors as rats and lice ate away their clothes. During the summer they struggled to survive 100-degree heat;[34] in the winter they nearly froze.

But they had the Scriptures with them, for Prem had read the Bible multiple times as a new believer. He knew the Word by heart and led the prisoners through the Bible from beginning to end three times that year. Those in surrounding cells listened. Prem's first disciples grew up behind bars.

---

34 Fahrenheit (37 degrees Celsius)

Prem would be arrested and thrown into prison many more times. During one of his prison sentences, he was forced to stay in a small, cave-like chamber reserved for the bodies of those who died in prison until their families could retrieve their corpses. Prem could not stand up or stretch out in the cramped cell. The authorities expected him to die or go insane within one week, but Prem sang to Jesus and envisioned the Scriptures.

Several weeks later, a guard approached the cell and heard talking. "Who are you talking to?" the guard yelled.

"Jesus," Prem answered.

The guard shone his flashlight into the cell. "Where is Jesus? I don't see Him here."

"You can't find Him that way," Prem said. "Let me show you how to find Him." Prem shared the gospel with the guard, and he believed.

PREM'S WITNESS SPREADS

Prem was still alive after spending five months in the corpse chamber. Jesus kept him company and saved his life as people slipped him food. Eventually, the authorities moved Prem to another prison—out of solitary confinement and into a cell with other people.

"I know a Man," he kept saying, "who died and rose again."

Prem was moved again and again—14 prisons in 10 years—and in each place he spoke of the Lord Jesus. Men from dozens of tribes heard the gospel and believed. When these men were released, they returned to their homes and villages, spreading the gospel to every province in Nepal.

When Prem was released, he did what the Lord showed him to do: he built an orphanage and a school, and adopted 100 children. Schools did not exist in the mountains, and he wanted to raise children to know the Lord Jesus and be educated so they could advance in life and spread the gospel. When those 100 children grew up, many became missionaries.

The price paid early—the seed planted—has produced much fruit today.

APPENDIX TWO

TESTIMONY STORIES OF CHRISTIANS ASSOCIATED WITH
PHILEMON'S MINISTRY

CHITRA'S STORY

Here is the personal testimony of Chitra, whom I (the compiler of this book) met at our seminar in 2019. He was responsible for most of the logistical details for this event, attended by over 150 people from the region of Darjeeling around Siliguri. At the seminar, we also met others from their church and their children, many of whom were involved in the music ministry, and received their testimonies as well. The pattern of change and spontaneous witnessing to relatives and friends is striking.

Chitra is now pastor of a church in Siliguri and also headmaster of a government school, married to Sarita, and father to a teenage daughter (sixteen) and son (fifteen).

Chitra was a smart student and read voluminously in many fields while he was in high school and college. He was also on the way to demon worship, reading about black magic at the time he met Philemon. Philemon would share about the Gospels and encourage Chitra to read the Bible. Chitra's first impression was how smiling and happy Philemon appeared to be.

While Chitra's parents were Hindus, he knew something of Christian thought from some relatives who were Christians. He was quick to challenge Philemon's Biblical teachings based on philosophies from his readings and Hindu background, but Philemon would only say "Let's pray about it" in answer to any objections. Slowly, it became apparent to Chitra that Christ was real. Meanwhile, he worshipped many gods and prayed to them while adding Jesus to their number. His discussions with Philemon went on for some time.

During this time, Chitra had been feeling more frustrated and depressed with the challenges that came along with being nineteen and finishing twelfth grade. He found himself thinking dark thoughts and considering suicide.

Then one night he decided this was it. He didn't like poison as a solution and was thinking how else he would end his life when his friend's father, a local Hindu man (still unsaved at time of writing), grabbed him by the arm and made him come along to a spiritual conference Philemon was putting on. Chitra resisted, but this man obligated him to go along because he felt he could not attend by himself.

That night, the preacher said during his closing prayer, "There is a young man in the left back corner to whom the devil is lying, telling him to kill himself. But he will receive a new horizon if he will repent and believe in Jesus." Chitra took note of this and knew the prophecy was meant for him. Although he believed that Jesus was real, he did not yet completely yield his life to Jesus. He was still too stubborn to yield, but he put away the thought of suicide after the preacher prophesied for him.

His life was not smooth. He returned to college, tried to concentrate on his studies and be happy with friends, but his inner self was restless. He also heard some strange voices which he now knows were voices from the dark world. Those voices would tell him things about other people. He was struggling inside, and also losing his sanity. It's also said that someone had tried to put a spirit over him. Finally, Chitra confessed his problems to Philemon, who prayed over him with concern.

Six months after the initial experience with the preacher, Philemon took Chitra to another meeting. Feeling the need to be converted, he went forward. At this meeting, seven or eight pastors prayed for him and he felt something leaving him. On the way home, he noted that his mind was free of the heaviness he had experienced for the last years.

And so the discussion that lasted almost three years bore fruit, and Chitra was baptized about two months later. He says now that head and Bible knowledge was not enough, but he eventually yielded to Jesus Himself.

Persecution followed this decision.

Chitra's older brothers somehow found out what had happened through the spirits they worshipped. The second brother was quite rough on him when he went back home. He said, "You are now low caste—an untouchable, and no longer a brother! Come home only as a guest."

So Chitra left and got a room, but he no longer had any support to live on. And so he and Philemon prayed in faith, "God will provide."

God provided Chitra the idea to buy a camera, and so he bought a good used one and began to take pictures. It was the in thing at the time, and so he had customers, even though he was very inexperienced at first. He would make a profit of over 30% of the price. This provided his rent and college tuition and books for a number of years.

Meanwhile, Chitra's mother accepted Christ after a while. His younger brother is about to get baptized, along with his wife and son. Other family members received Jesus shortly after the mother, and most are now Christians.

So Chitra was the first in the family but many followed. In that town, the saying became that to be special one needed to "be like Philemon or like Bikele" (the headmaster).

Sarita was nine when she met Philemon's family in 1983. They were friends of her parents, and she spent a fair bit of time with them. Her mother was a Christian, and in 1988 her father became one too.

And so it came to be that her marriage to Chitra was arranged by her mother and "elder brother" Philemon, who also performed Sarita and Chitra's wedding.

Anil, a brother of Sarita, also became a Christian. He now leads a singing group at Chitra's church, and his son was the drummer at a recent seminar with speakers that included Philemon's Canadian friends. Besides this, Anil is involved in holistic health and counselling, working on spiritual, social and emotional healing as a medical ambassador, youth pastor, and music leader.

He had spent some time in a Christian hostel at five years of age, and was guided in that Christian environment, which was run by a Christian pastor and his son, who taught the Bible along with school subjects.

Anil had a bicycle accident at fourteen with a car driven by a drunk driver, but ended up with only scratches even though it drove over him. He thought of Revelation 3:20 and decided it was time to accept Jesus. Later, he felt called into the ministry, which he has been faithful in serving.

Anil's wife, Sarizar, relates that she came from a strict Hindu family in West Bengal. The family would worship every morning and only eat after these ceremonies (Puja). Her father drank heavily, so there was no peace in the family.

In grade two, she began to have a problem: she could not eat fruit or anything more than a little fish, or she would vomit. The doctor could not find anything wrong, but the problem continued.

About that time, an older women in her area who was a strong believer shared some food with her. Sarizar didn't want to eat, but this believer said the food would be okay as it had been prayed over. So Sarizar ate, and nothing happened this time. As a result, she allowed the lady to start teaching her and began studying the Bible with her. After she became a believer, the food problem disappeared.

Once her family found out, they said, "No, you can't go to study with this woman." But she still went—and eventually they did too, and all were baptized together. After a year, she began to share in this woman's witness and teaching ministry, and is still in ministry today in the same local church.

CHURCH PLANTING AND AREA SUPERVISORS TO PRAY FOR

Philemon's ministry extends to many areas of Nepal and North India through area supervisors like Habil. This section describes some of the work being carried out in these regions.

Lamahatta: This area around Darjeeling presently has twelve churches plus two schools in the original ministry area. Some of these operate under the supervision of Depcha. Others, including the Sherpa school (primary to grade five, where the whole community is involved) are under Pastor Pradeep. This is where Philemon started in the early seventies, and where some churches have moved on by joining other ministry associations that came later.

Northwest Bengal: Philemon knew Pradeep's father when he was in Sikkim, in the early seventies. Philemon's friend took him to meet Pradeep's father in a room where there were many implements used for magic and witchcraft. This man was sick and totally paralyzed, and two preachers came to preach the Gospel and pray deliverance for him, leading him to accept Christ and reject his magic. Pradeep's father started to preach and later moved to the northern part of West Bengal, where there were many Sherpas.

His son Pradeep attended that school, then helped his father run it, and has been in charge since his father died. Pradeep also started five or six churches in the area. Now he is in Siliguri. When a church with which he was associated lost its minister, he ended up taking on that responsibility too, in addition to working with all these churches and acting as area supervisor.

Earlier, Rhim was the supervisor in this area, but he wanted to work independently. He has joined another organization since, bringing along the churches he was working with. So while financial support to him has been discontinued, there are still mentoring connections in the spiritual ministry with him.

Jhapa area, Nepal: Subhan started seven churches some time ago. In the beginning, his neighbours almost killed him and chased him out of his village, so he left and went down to Jhapa. But slowly, he continued in the village which was his hometown, and the Lord worked in hearts until a church was established there. Subhan goes back to encourage them from time to time.

Subhan how has another five or six churches in Jhapa, which is an unreached area. He has become independent in support, but agreed to continue under the mentorship of Philemon. He has the gift of evangelism and has preached in open areas since he was a young believer.

Dhading area, west of Kathmandu, Nepal: There are six churches in Dhading, Nepal, under Bahadur. This is a fairly large area located in the hills, with several peaks around 7000 metres in the area.

Solukhumbu remote area, Nepal high hills: In Nepal, there is a small plain across the south, which quickly becomes sharply rising foothills up to 3300 metres (something like the area just before Banff in Canada), then the high hills and then the mountains, which include fourteen of the highest twenty peaks in the world. Mount Everest at 8850 metres is in this area.

The former supervisor here went to a foreign country to do some work. So Bandhu (a friend) has taken up the reins and presently has three churches. He was a student at one of Philemon's Bible schools. He was helping the senior pastor there, and when that pastor left the area, he took care of the work and ministry in the area on his own. The principle Philemon follows is that the one who is faithful and trusted is then entrusted with the supervision task after consultation, as study groups grow into churches.

Dolakha, Gaurishankar area, a bit further west from Solukhumba: A man named Prem (not Prem Pradhan) is presently supervising this church and area. His father was an elder who was involved with Philemon's uncle, who started the work in this area, including leading Philemon and his father to the Lord. Many in the area became Christians, and several other tribes were also evangelized. Other Christian groups have worked in this area as well since that time.

A HINDU FAMILY STORY FROM CHITRA'S CONGREGATION

Monal was a young student working to enter university around 2010. All of his family members were Hindu at that time, and he was fervently against Jesus. But in his last years in high school, he developed insomnia and couldn't sleep properly for several years.

Some Christians told him Jesus was Lord of all. He didn't believe it, but he was in big trouble. He was turning to drugs and alcohol to cope with his weariness. As time went by, he was not able to get his entrance to university. He was studying hard, but struggling due to the lack of proper sleep. He called upon his gods for help. Nothing.

One night, in desperation, he prayed, "Jesus, if You are the Son of God, Lord of all, then show me Your power to help me sleep." That night, for the first night in years, he slept all night.

It was clear to him that Jesus had done it, but he didn't surrender his life to Him right away. He slept the next night, and the next, and the next, and the next. What a change! He started to read the Gospels and take them seriously. As he read with a new sincerity, he came to see that Jesus was the one and only Son of God, the Lord over all creation.

He gave up his reliance on the many Hindu gods who had not helped him. He gave his soul to the One who had died for him, like the first Christians in Thessalonica did. He *"turned to God from idols to serve the living and true God, and to wait for his Son from heaven, whom he raised from the dead—Jesus, who rescues us from the coming wrath"* (1 Thessalonians 1:9–10, NIV).

Immediately, all his relatives were watching him sleep. Not only did the Lord give him sleep every night now for ten years, but He also conquered his bad habits of drugs and booze, of which his relatives were all aware and unhappy. As he continued to study the Word of God, the Lord changed him completely. Everyone saw the great changes, but in anger his Hindu parents cut off all financial support for his further education.

One day, as he went again to see if his university entrance permit would be given, the Lord had a surprise for him. Suddenly his mind was filled with a clear thought. "Today you will go to the school and be turned away again, but then you will be accepted back and given your entrance permit." It happened exactly that way. The first official told him to come back in a few days. As he walked off the grounds, his cellphone rang. A second official in the admissions office told him to come and get his entrance permit. He was stunned and thankful. It was a great encouragement at that point, since he was the only Christian in his extended family, and all his aunts and uncles were against him for breaking up the unity of the family and dishonouring the Hindu gods by turning from them.

Although Monal's uncle was also very upset with him, he talked often about Jesus with his pre-adolescent cousin. The Lord opened her heart. She was very close with her mom and shared her new joy in Christ immediately. Her parents were very near divorce because her dad was so tough and hard. Her mom responded to the Lord Jesus, who had all power yet was so tender, compassionate, and loving to those in need, but she avoided speaking with her husband in a way that would create more tension. However, in Monal's cousin's new joy and enthusiasm for discovering the truth about Christ, she repeatedly spoke with confidence in Jesus to her father. Mother and daughter learned to fast and pray for him. He was so aggressive and hard, but to everyone's amazement, the Lord made his heart soft, and he went to a meeting and there turned away from the Hindu gods to call on Jesus as the one Saviour of sinners.

On the verge of divorce, suddenly the person who was the key problem in the marriage was a new man. Now there were two happy women in the house and a happy man! This was utterly astounding to their family and relatives. Over the next ten years, twenty-five of Monal's family members have turned from Hinduism to embrace the love and power of the one true God and His Son, Jesus Christ, including his parents!

Today, Monal's uncle, aunt, and cousin love to praise the Lord together with him in music. The Lord of the Bible, God the Father, Son, and Spirit, is the one true God, and *He* is good! And He's not finished saving more relatives!

JESUS SAVES WITCH DOCTORS TOO

Another testimony of another kind: from the tea garden area in the high hills of Gorubathan. This story illustrates the spiritual battles that are part of the evangelization of remote areas where Philemon and his team have worked. Even the larger centres in these areas were villages along trails that were accessible sometimes by bus but mainly by walking during Philemon's early ministry.

In 2019, I (the compiler) met an elder of a local church, who works in the local tea factory across the road from his home. Outside, this looks a bit like a cedar-covered home like mine, but there is only one layer of overlapping boards, and the building is not large, with four small rooms. Across the room, we were introduced to a lively but older man and woman, the parents of the elder, as well as some other family members and later, neighbours.

This man came to Christ just over ten years ago. He was the head witch doctor in the area.

Dhonnu dealt with the monkey god, Shiva, and many other gods, and Tibetan spirit gods as well. He talked to them, and because of their power, he could see diseases and to know the demons that caused them. He said he could even heal broken bones in half an hour with incantations.

Then one day a lady with a broken tailbone asked him to visit her after trying other witch doctors in other places and even a hospital over three weeks. She was to the point of not being able to move. He went and said, "I can fix it, but why did you wait?" He spent five minutes using some demonic mantras, then went on to his appointment with his job until that afternoon.

The woman's daughter called and reported that she had started walking again with a stick. More mantras, and then she could walk normally again. Each day after visiting, the then-witch doctor would go to his field, work for the day, cut grass for his cows in the evening, and then go home.

His back was cold the second day, and this continued for two weeks. He then asked his spirit about this cold, and the spirit said not to worry as it would be healed.

But the next day he became seriously sick, and the day after that, his fingers were swollen. He could no longer walk properly, and he fell many times. He was upset, as the spirit had implied healing in hours; was he lying? In his words,

> I was angry with this spirit that lived in the bigger temple on my yard, who at the time spoke to me face to face. I became very weak the next day, feeling like I would die. At this point I remembered that I'd heard that Jesus could heal people. So I said in my head, "If you can save me, I will follow."
>
> I slept again, and in my dream I saw a bright thing like white light that brought happiness. When I woke up, my fingers were back to normal again. So I thought, "Maybe Jesus can actually save." Then again I said, "I will follow. But it must happen without medicine."
>
> I slept yet again, and had the same dreams and joy. Because I was feeling better, I sent my wife to call a local pastor called Philemon [not the man described in this book] and he came and prayed. I started shivering. I could not control my body but I spoke continuously, arms out, jumping, "I am Jesus; I have done so much for you."
>
> The pastor said, "The spirit in you isn't Jesus. He doesn't jump like that. This is an evil spirit." But the pastor could not cast him out. And so some people from Siliguri—Pastor Danzig and Chitra's son—came here, and threw all my idols, a special staff, and other items from my temple into the river with my permission. Then I kicked my temple in the house and said to the spirit, "You can't do anything to me." The spirits began to leave me with the prayers of these men.

After this, Dhonnu went to the Siliguri church while it was holding a big meeting. The believers formed a circle around

Dhonnu and prayed for him. Again, some spirits left, but there were still some that stayed. More prayer followed, and then Dhonnu prayed and fasted for three days for deliverance. He felt he had received the new birth and the Holy Spirit, but that a particularly bad spirit was hiding in a box in his house.

In his dreams he saw three strong people who looked muscular and dangerous. He told us, "The next day, my son took that box outside and burned it. The next evening I saw two spirits leave, but one was left. That one was torturing my wife as well. His head was spinning and his leg got weak, but after much prayer he was healed."

This was the testimony of his deliverance and coming to Jesus in 2007. He has been a disciple and strong supporter of Christianity in his area ever since.

Together with the Philemon of this story, a team from Canada met this man, now 87, in early 2019. We were asked to pray for him and his wife. A spirit, sometimes manifesting as a water buffalo and sometimes as a strong man, was causing problems in his house, and was bothering his wife when asked to leave. Dhonnu had been spending much time praying about this matter, but was requesting help.

Philemon spent quite some time reminding Dhonnu of the scriptural framework of his position in Christ, and then prayed protection against this spirit—first for the wife, who calmed almost immediately, and then for her husband, and to break off any power in that place and house, and the area around it.

I felt led to speak about faithfulness bringing freedom from John 5, and about putting our sights on Jesus (Colossians 3:1) as the solution to putting off the old man. I felt reminded that Satan does not like to let go, and sometimes brings back on old temptation years later. I also prayed, and our team prayed along with us in their hearts as we put our hands on these dear people.

This is an area with an influential Buddhist association in the area. Others in this family came to the Lord about 2006. Pastor Danzig (presently the senior pastor at the church where the 2019 conference was held) was involved in leading some to the Lord. What started as praying for the health of one Buddhist who was the president of the association at the time, became the gradual coming to Christ of the rest of the family. This happened even though the Tamang tribe and the Buddhist association both excommunicated the first one to accept Jesus. They invited him many times to remain associated with them as a Buddhist who had added Jesus to his personal pantheon of gods, but he knew Jesus is the only way, and must be worshiped as the supreme and only God.

CORE VISION AND MINISTRY OF ENGAGE TODAY

The vision of ENGAGE is to build mutually beneficial relationships between churches in Canada and indigenous missions that result in:

a. the mobilization of indigenous missions to reach the remaining unreached peoples with the Gospel
b. the Church in the West gaining a renewed passion and vision for mission

BRIEF OVERVIEW OF ENGAGE TODAY

It is estimated that over 2 billion have not yet heard the true Gospel of Jesus Christ. They are "without hope and without God in the world." They are those who we call the unreached. Engage Today (ENGAGE) was established in order that Christ be proclaimed to the remaining unreached.

God has blessed the Church in the West with abundant resources, extensive Biblical training, and freedom to travel. On the one hand, we in the West offer the Church in the non-West help and support in fulfilling the Great Commission. On the other hand, the Church in the non-West is our example of zeal, flexibility, and persistence. This is interdependency. ENGAGE has made it our primary goal to build relationships between the Church in Canada and emerging indigenous missions in the least reached regions of the world. These relationships bring mutual encouragement for the glory of God.

ENGAGE partners with dynamic, indigenous Christian leaders who have established what we call indigenous missions. An indigenous mission is an organization led by someone reaching their own people group with the Gospel. These leaders have a vision for God to be glorified among their people. They demonstrate faithfulness in the face of relentless opposition. They are accountable in their partnership with ENGAGE. They are examples of humbly serving with Biblical childlike faith. It is our privilege to come alongside these servants of God.

ENGAGE currently partners with twenty mission leaders in five countries—India, Bangladesh, Myanmar, Nepal, and Indonesia—who oversee over 850 local indigenous staff. Their ministries are steadily bearing fruit through disciple-making. Baptisms are regular events for our partners. These missions have planted thousands of churches.

ABOUT OUR PARTNERSHIPS

The key priority which characterizes all of our partnerships is a vision to bring the hope of the Gospel of Jesus Christ to the unreached. Some of our partners have a focus on sending and supporting workers where Christ is not known. Other partners emphasize training and preparing missionaries with the same focus.

Engage Today values our partners, and we evaluate our work by asking ourselves: "Are we serving them well?" Our desire is to strengthen the work that God has called them to. This involves a variety of activities, including pastoral care, teaching and encouragement, financial support, and, not least, prayer. Relationship is the context through which we carry out these foci.

Pastoral care usually takes the shape of walking closely with our partners. Often this involves travelling to spend time with them or inviting them to Canada to connect with us and believers in Canada. These leaders typically don't have anyone to confide in where they are located, and so we commonly serve as pastors for them.

Teaching and encouragement are things our partners often tell us that they lack. Very few have the opportunity to receive formal Bible training. Pastors often are commissioned with the heart and vision for mission but with little to no preparation. Additionally, many pastors/missionaries serve in remote and challenging places. Encouragement is needed to persevere.

ENGAGE has been active in bringing together indigenous missionaries and pastors for Bible training and encouragement through our Leadership Seminar ministry. Teams from Canada travel to where these frontline servants can gather together for a multi-day conference in a camp-like setting.

ENGAGE also assists partners who have established their own Bible schools to prepare and equip more missionaries. Often this takes the shape of financial support because students and local churches are not able to support the operation of these schools.

The main emphasis for financial support is based in ENGAGE's vision for interdependency. In the West, we are the "haves" and our brothers and sisters in the Non-West are the "have nots." Pastors and missionaries coming from non-Christian backgrounds do not have a local support network to help them conduct their ministry. This is the case for most of our brothers and sisters. ENGAGE gives Canadians the opportunity to come alongside front-line missionaries, enabling them to carry out their work by providing financial support in the context of mission partnership.

ENGAGE also advocates for financial support to equip our partners with the tools they need for their ministry. Transportation vehicles such as bicycles or motorcycles are often a key need for pastors to travel to the many villages they are ministering in. Equipping them with Bibles and literature is commonly a key need as well.

From time to time there are emergencies and disasters which necessitate a compassionate response. Although this is not the major emphasis of our ministry, we seek to respond in a way that is proportional to our other ministerial financial support. Engage seeks to enable our partners to respond well with a faithful gospel witness in these circumstances.

Prayer is the heartbeat of all our work. We recognize our dependence on the Lord and that it is only by His grace that anything which is done will have eternal value.

Through relationship and connection, ENGAGE is seeking to build a well-informed, intimate context through which the people of God are praying. We want people to be close to our partners so that praying for them is a central part of the relationship.

ENGAGE believes that linking Canadians with indigenous missions in partnership will result in unreached peoples being reached with the Gospel and Canadians experiencing revival through following in obedience to the call of Christ on His Church.

LIGHT SHINING
INTO DARKNESS

You light a lamp for me. The Lord, my God, lights up my darkness.

—Psalm 18:28, NLT

Light shines in the darkness for the godly. They are generous, compassionate, and righteous.

—Psalm 112:4, NLT

Your word is a lamp to guide my feet and a light for my path.

—Psalm 119:105, NLT

...the people who sat in darkness have seen a great light. And for those who lived in the land where death casts its shadow, a light has shined.

—Matthew 4:16, NLT

The Word gave life to everything that was created, and his life brought light to everyone. The light shines in the darkness, and the darkness can never extinguish it.

—John 1:4-5, NLT

I have come as a light to shine in this dark world, so that all who put their trust in me will no longer remain in the dark.

—John 12:46, NLT

For God, who said, "Let there be light in the darkness," has made this light shine in our hearts so we could know the glory of God that is seen in the face of Jesus Christ.

We now have this light shining in our hearts, but we ourselves are like fragile clay jars containing this great treasure. This makes it clear that our great power is from God, not from ourselves.

—2 Corinthians 4:6–7, NLT

Because of that experience, we have even greater confidence in the message proclaimed by the prophets. You must pay close attention to what they wrote, for their words are like a lamp shining in a dark place—until the Day dawns, and Christ the Morning Star shines in your hearts.

—2 Peter 1:19, NLT